How
To Hold You

How I Came To Hold You

Ben Wakeling

"Heartbreaking and heartwarming…
these stories embody tradgedy, hope and love."
Kym Lomas

Matador
9 Priory Business Park,
Wistow Road, Kibworth Beauchamp,
Leicestershire. LE8 0RX
Tel: (+44) 116 279 2299
Fax: (+44) 116 279 2277
Email: books@troubador.co.uk
Web: www.troubador.co.uk/matador

ISBN 978 1780885 681

British Library Cataloguing in Publication Data.
A catalogue record for this book is available from the British Library.

Typeset by Troubador Publishing Ltd, Leicester, UK
Printed and bound in Great Britain by
Clays Ltd, St Ives plc

Matador is an imprint of Troubador Publishing Ltd

To every parent who has empty arms.

Contents

When a spouse loses their significant other, they are referred to as a widow or widower.

When a child loses his or her parents, they are considered to be an orphan.

There is no name, title or word to describe a parent who has lost a child.

– Anon

Foreword

Tentative. That's how I'd describe the mood when my wife entered the kitchen brandishing a pregnancy test, complete with little blue cross. There was no jumping for joy, no rapturous cheers; just a man and his wife looking at each other with bulging eyes and one rather confused toddler, who stood between us, looking from one face to the other, wondering what on earth was going on.

I can't help but think that this is the reaction of most parents who have previously suffered the loss of a child, whether it be through miscarriage (as ours was, at eight weeks), stillbirth or neonatal death. It is a time of excitement, yet fear; joy, yet anxiety. Some have said they felt as if they were holding their breath for nine months, barely daring to hope that all will be well. *How I Came To Hold You* looks at these challenges and emotions in an attempt to demonstrate that there is life after death, that although grief never disappears it can live alongside happiness once again.

My wife and I were unaware of Sands, the stillbirth and neonatal death charity, when we suffered our loss, which is a huge shame. Having become more involved with their service and the wonderfully dedicated people who work, volunteer and fundraise for them, I increasingly wish that we had received their help during our darkest hours. The work they do is simply incredible, and so I thank you for buying this book and contributing to the funds that they plough into support, information and research.

My deepest thanks also go to every parent who has had the courage to open their hearts and mouths to me, sharing their stories for the benefit of other parents in a similar situation. You are all a testament to the resilience and strength of the human spirit. I hope that, through reading the experiences of others, bereaved parents can find some solace and comfort in the fact that they are not alone.

There is nothing more precious than a treasured memory.

Thank you again.

Ben Wakeling
September 2012

Hannah

It was 1993 when Martine Brennan left the buzz of London behind and travelled the five hundred miles to the town of Tralee, in County Kerry, to raise her first child in the beautiful surroundings of the Dingle Peninsula.

The pregnancy was difficult, not helped by moving countries at five months' gestation. Her nausea was not restricted to the morning; it had the audacity to rear its ugly head noon and night as well. Fortunately, she was blessed with a short labour, and gave birth at home without any pain relief; the only blip was when the contractions and pains stopped halfway through childbirth. Not to be deterred from the task at hand, Martine whiled away the time by eating jelly and listening to Ray Charles.

Finally, her daughter was born. "I felt ten feet tall when she arrived," recollects Martine. She named her daughter Aine, the name borne by the Queen of the Fairies in Celtic mythology. It means 'brightness, or radiance' – and she certainly lived up to her name: "She stared right up into my eyes, and she was so beautiful."

It was ten years before Martine would become pregnant again. She and Gerard had been trying for what seemed like an age, but to no avail; in fact, Martine had almost given up hope when one day a home test gave a positive result. She remembers it well: "Gerard and I just cried when the lines came up."

Unlike her first pregnancy, this time there was no nausea; but Martine's baby kept having horrible hiccups, which bothered her. Then, inexplicably, at around seven months, Martine lost half a stone in weight.

As with many parents, Martine had been told that the first three months of pregnancy was the 'danger period'. She was aware of the risk of miscarriage, but had been told very little about stillbirth. And so, once fourteen weeks were passed, she thought that she and her baby were safe. In addition to this, Martine had been told by health professionals that her baby's movements would lessen towards the end of her pregnancy. Looking back, Martine feels this contributed to her not realising that her unborn baby – another daughter, named Hannah – was in difficulty. "Mothers should be taught to count the baby's kicks," she asserts.

Her worst fears were confirmed after she went to hospital following sharp abdominal pains. She hadn't felt her baby move during the past day, and subsequent scans showed that Hannah had, tragically, died.

Martine and Gerard were sent home from hospital to wait for labour to start naturally. Four days later, unable to bear the wait, Martine asked to be induced. When she went to hospital, she was told to rest on the ward, where mothers were giving birth to healthy babies. "This was barbaric," recalls Martine, "and I refused. Our relationship with the hospital midwife went downhill after that."

Hannah was born asleep at thirty-two weeks on a Thursday night in a private room, the cord wrapped three times around her neck. Gerard was by Martine's side: "He was amazing," remembers Martine, fondly. "He was with me through it all."

Martine and Gerard stayed with Hannah all night. Gerard

cuddled her, whilst an exhausted and weak Martine attempted to recover from the worst experience of her life. In the morning, close family arrived to offer their support and love.

It was three days after Hannah's birth, when Martine and Gerard discovered – by chance – that they could take her home. For three days they held her and talked to her in the family home, giving her all the love they had. Family and close friends came round; one of them gave a private Mass. Martine and Gerard carried her coffin in their arms as they travelled to the graveyard, where they buried Hannah alongside her grandparents.

Martine had terrible nightmares during the first few weeks following Hannah's birth that her lost daughter was being taken away on a bus, Martine held back and prevented from going with her. She would wake up screaming, and pace the floor at 2am every night. For weeks she was unable to go into Hannah's room, or touch her things. She found it difficult to visit her daughter's grave, going with Gerard once a week.

No-one asked Gerard how he was feeling. Everyone who approached him asked after Martine: how she was, whether she was coping, how she was feeling. He visited Hannah's grave a lot, grieving quietly in between working and looking after his wife and daughter.

"I felt I had to take care of the family first, that my own grief had to take second place," he recalls. "I had to be strong for both of us."

Out of the ashes of despair rose the flames of love. Whilst tragedy can often tear a family in two, Martine and Gerard clung to each other, and were rarely apart. They told Aine – who was ten years old at the time – that her sister would not be coming home to stay; that they didn't know why she had died.

3

"I felt like a leper," remembers Martine, adding that she lost touch with most of her friends, who avoided her – and the subject. Those who did speak to her offered misplaced words of condolence. "They often said, 'You have a little angel in Heaven now'. This made me very angry."

Why? Because neither Martine nor Gerard wanted an angel in Heaven. They wanted a baby, a girl that they could hold and love. Martine felt that Hannah was her gift from God, a reflection of the meaning of her name. But this gift had been taken from them so cruelly, and as a result Martine's faith suffered. "I had a very strong faith before Hannah died," says Martine, "now I feel very unsure. My old way of believing doesn't work anymore and I haven't yet figured out what to put in its place."

Whilst some people gave misplaced words of advice, others went out of their way to avoid Martine and her family. One day she was walking through her local supermarket, and saw an acquaintance. The acquaintance, in turn, spotted her and, like a frightened rabbit, ducked behind a tall aisle. Presumably she remained in this hunched form for a while, scurrying around behind her trolley, for Martine didn't see her again. "It took me a few minutes to realise that she was hiding from me," chuckles Martine. "I didn't know whether to laugh or cry!"

The only people who understood were those who had suffered a similar tragedy. Martine found comfort and support in the arms of her close family: Gerard, Aine and her sister. It made Hannah feel more 'real' to her, and she was not under pressure to recover, to 'get over it' – a comfort not demonstrated by everyone, as Martine recalls: "I think most people became fed up with me when I wasn't 'getting over it' after about five months."

A few things helped Martine cope with the grief of losing her daughter. Friends called round to her house each week and listened to her talk about Hannah. She started a diary to record her feelings and emotions, which later became the basis for her book *From Out of the Darkness*, which took nearly six years to finish. One thing kept riling Martine, though: the careless and hurtful actions of the hospital midwife.

It was bad enough that Martine was almost forced to share a ward with mothers in labour and giving birth to healthy babies; but the midwife's throwaway comments were akin to rubbing salt in the wound. "You have a baby at home," she said, as if Aine was some form of consolation prize after Hannah's death. In the weeks following their loss, Martine and Gerard received a phone call from a public health nurse. The reason for phoning? "She said she needed to 'check me off the list'."

The most helpful words were the simplest. No sugar-coating, no attempt at flowery language. It was simply that Martine and Gerard would always miss their baby, but that – with time – the pain would ease. Every year, on Hannah's birthday, Martine and her family write her name in the sand on the shores of Ireland and release balloons in her memory. It is a time for sharing stories about Hannah, for support and unity as a family. Martine's most treasured memory of Hannah, however, involves just the two of them: when she held her daughter in her arms and sang to her whilst no-one else was there.

*

Martine and Gerard started trying for another baby as soon as possible after Hannah's death; and, just after Hannah's first birthday, Martine discovered that she was pregnant with her third child. This time, there were no tears of joy. "I was terrified," says Martine – a terror which lasted for nine months. "The fear never left me until I heard Caoimhe's first cry." It was not just the fear that Martine would have to suffer the death of another child that worried her; it was that she would lose her mind if another daughter was lost.

"There was no great rejoicing this time," remembers Martine, when recalling how friends and family reacted after hearing the news. "I think we all had a wait and see, hope and pray approach."

Her fears were, unfortunately, not alleviated by the hospital staff. Every time Martine and Gerard attended an appointment, they had to recall the story of Hannah's death and birth. At one point, Martine refused – everything that the midwives, doctors and sonographers needed to know was in her notes – but she was told she could not have her check-up until she had retold the same painful story that had been uttered countless times before. One health professional asked Martine if she was still breastfeeding Hannah; another professional, this time a sonographer, thought that an extra ultrasound requested by Martine to ensure that all was well was to see if Caoimhe had Down's Syndrome.

Martine's approach to pregnancy was vastly different to that of her previous children. "I was afraid to exercise," she recollects. "I didn't gather baby clothes or make plans. I was constantly aware of Caoimhe's movements. I didn't sleep much."

For many, pregnancy is a joyful time; but not for Martine. "I was afraid to be happy," she says, "in case Caoimhe didn't survive." She monitored Caoimhe's heartbeat constantly, and asked her home birth midwife for extra heartbeat checks. She would happily have worn a monitor for twenty-four hours a day, she remarks.

Joyfully, Caoimhe survived the pregnancy, and was born

without intervention or pain relief in a birthing pool situated in the kitchen. Martine had her eyes squeezed shut until she heard the sound she so desperately longed for: Caoimhe's first cry. "The relief was enormous," she recalls affectionately. "I kept asking the midwife if Caoimhe was OK."

Losing a child changes things. It changes a parent's perception of a subsequent pregnancy, replacing joy with fear. It turns the miracle of childbirth into a time of anxiety. But, perhaps most of all, it changes a parent's outlook on life.

"I believe strongly now in the saying 'Seize the day'," says Martine. "Life is too short to put off being with people we love and doing the things that make us happy."

When people ask how many children she has, Martine says she has three beautiful daughters. If she is having a good day, she mentions that one of them died in 2004. Just because Hannah is not around doesn't mean she isn't real.

Her family is closer now than it has ever been. They laugh a lot, says Martine. They celebrate the little things; and, although they remember Hannah with sadness, they talk about her often, and with deep love.

"We have learned that it is still possible for us to be happy and enjoy our life even though we miss Hannah. But I know now how fragile life is."

An Excerpt From
From Out of the Darkness
by Martine Brennan

Dear Hannah,

The days have been better now for a while. I have begun to work again. I know now that it is possible to survive, to feel interested in life again. But what a painful road this has been, each step carved out of dogged determination. Old beliefs lie wasted along the roadside. Old friends a memory, and the gratitude I used to feel decimated.

I thought I would die… but I didn't. I thought I would be the woman I used to be again… but I am not. I understand now that every day I make a choice to live. I understand that life does not stand still or stop because you are not here so I move, I learn, I live. I still have all the questions and no answers. I have learned to live with them all, my constant companions. I live in the unknowing every single day. I live with the loss of you, my lovely wee girl.

I don't need to talk about you so much anymore. I hold you close in my heart, always loving you as I live my life once again. I look around and I see the beauty in a flower. I go for walks and can hear and enjoy the birds singing. I can sleep at night and wake rested. I can work now knowing it is always possible to find another way. I can laugh again.

8

I have learned that we are all far more resilient than we think we are. I found courage and I found strength. And in the end I found joy. I am so glad I had you, even for just a little while.

Hannah, you are forever a part of me now.

Francesca

Maria Riley became pregnant about a year after she married Chris, a work colleague, in a beautiful winter wedding. They'd always said they wanted a baby together – Maria had two children, Nathan and Antonia, from a previous marriage, and the newlyweds felt that one of their own would bond the new family. It seemed that their dream had become reality, and – in a departure from tradition – it was Chris who held the pregnancy test, spending the nail-biting few minutes waiting for the blue lines to appear.

Appear they did, and the ensuing nine months went well; however, labour was far from straightforward. "Having Beau was quite a horrific experience," says Chris, adding that his son came out at "a rate of knots". As a result, Maria suffered massive haemorrhaging.

It was a frantic time. After three hours of surgery, Maria awoke in intensive care. One of the midwives who had helped deliver Beau entered the room. "She said I'd lost half of my blood," remembers Maria, "and that they'd gone home thinking there was going to be a fatality. They said if I'd had him at home I wouldn't be here today."

The experience was so terrible for both Chris and Maria that it was five years before they tried for another. "We only intended to have the one," says Maria, "but Beau went to school; and, suddenly, we had a quiet, empty house."

And so, in March 2009, Maria became pregnant with her fourth child. Being thirty-eight at the time, she was always aware that she fell under the 'high risk' category, and as such was susceptible to a number of pregnancy-related conditions. Although she knew that the chance of foetal abnormality or miscarriage was high, she was quietly confident. "Because I'd had three children before, you kind of take it for granted that everything's going to be fine."

However, her worst fears were realised, and the twelve-week scan showed that there was a problem. This came as a shock to them both – an experience exacerbated by a sonographer who was painfully blunt. "We picked the bad one," recalls Maria. "She just looked, and straightaway said: 'There's something wrong with the head'."

The scan showed that her baby's head was surrounded by what looked like a bubble. After a consultation with a midwife counsellor, Maria and Chris were sent to Birmingham Women's Hospital for a chorionic villus sampling (CVS) test: a collection of cells, removed from the placenta, and tested for genetic defects.

A subsequent ultrasound scan at Birmingham showed that Maria and Chris' baby had cystic hygroma – a bulge at the base of the neck. Ordinarily, the bulge should measure three millimetres; in Maria's case, it measured ten. The CVS sample was sent for testing, and the anxious parents went home.

For two days they waited for the phone call which would tell them whether or not their baby had a genetic defect. How was the wait? "Dreadful," recalls Maria. "You wait until your twelve-week scan before you tell anybody, so nobody knew."

Finally, the call came: all clear. The good news was that the baby had no chromosomal defects; the bad was that the results were inconclusive. Whilst relieved, Chris and Maria were unsure of the future. Was there still a problem? Should they tell people outside close friends and family?

Over the next few weeks, Chris and Maria's baby underwent further tests, each with its own agonising wait for the results. "It's the wait that kills you," recollects Maria. "We just didn't know what to do." At twenty weeks, staff checked for heart defects: again, the results were all clear, but now the doctors were concerned that there was a problem with the brain, and so Maria was sent for an MRI scan at her local hospital.

This time, there was a two week wait for results. Maria recalls the experience with dark humour: "How I didn't go grey over night, I don't know." Neither she nor Chris could relax and enjoy the pregnancy. When they told their children that they would have a new brother or sister, there were no great celebrations, just excitement – especially amongst the younger children. Beau was ecstatic; Antonia was desperate for a little sister to play with.

Antonia would have to wait to see if her wish for a sister would come true: Chris and Maria had earlier decided that they would not find out the sex of their baby, despite the numerous tests being able to conclusively confirm whether they were having a boy or girl. However, despite being resolute that they would wait before finding out the sex, they were betrayed by a printed copy of recent results.

"We noticed on the top of the printout that it said 'XX46'," says Maria, "so we were like: 'Oh, she's female'." Being fond of unusual names, they named her Francesca, meaning 'free'. "We both really wanted that name," remembers Maria, fondly.

Francesca's brain scan results came through, and were again inconclusive. Chris and Maria found themselves shuttled back and forth between pieces of good and bad news, and were at the point where they needed a firm answer, so that they could deal with the repercussions.

Maria headed into the third trimester; and, for the first time during her pregnancy, gained weight – but for the wrong reasons. Tests revealed that she was suffering from polyhydramnios – an excess of amniotic fluid, which occurs in around one in 250 pregnancies, and is another sign of a foetal abnormality. Placed on a course of tablets, it began to subside; but scans were revealing that Francesca had a slight amount of fluid on one of her lungs, an amount which increased during each fortnightly appointment.

On the morning of her thirty-six-week appointment, Maria attended an assembly at her daughter's school; but her mind was elsewhere. Francesca's movements were less frequent.

"I just sat there, and all I could think was 'Come on, kick.' I could feel something, but they weren't hard, firm movements."

Maria remembers the look on the sonographer's face when her scan revealed a large black mass on the screen: the excess amniotic fluid was back with a vengeance. She and Chris were placed in a small side room whilst consultants reviewed the results of her scan. After a while, the Professor of Foetal Medicine entered, and dropped a bombshell: Francesca had to be delivered immediately.

Maria was prepared, and had already packed her overnight bags. Her mother's intuition had told her that something was wrong, and her mind turned to a close friend who had recently suffered the loss of a child following a diaphragmatic hernia. "She'd always said to me, 'One of us is going to come out with a baby'," remembers Maria. "The chances of it happening to both of us…"

Her waters were broken, and contractions began; but Francesca's heart rate was dipping, and so an emergency Caesarean section was scheduled. Eighteen minutes later, Francesca was born.

Almost immediately, Chris and Maria's new baby was surrounded by hospital staff. "That's where Chris came in as being supportive," says Maria. "He was just sitting by me, and I was saying 'Is she alright, is she alright?' You could see he'd got tears welling up in his eyes."

Maria was taken to a recovery room whilst Chris fetched the bags from the car. As he was away, a nurse entered and gave Maria the grave news: "She's very sick."

Francesca was filled with fluid, which the doctors and midwives were desperately trying to drain. Chris and Maria were taken to see her, an exhausted Maria still recovering from the effects of anaesthesia. "Chris was in bits," she recalls. "I remember feeling annoyed that I wasn't crying, or anything."

Their baby was in an incubator, and eight months after first being told there was a problem Chris and Maria finally had a firm diagnosis. Francesca was suffering from cystic hygroma and pleural effusions: a collection of fluid within the chest which constricts the lungs; lungs which the hospital staff informed the distraught parents were "not compatible with life".

"It really spells it out to you, doesn't it?" remembers Maria. "At that point, we thought, 'She's not going to make it'."

She and Chris spent the night in a private room, drifting in and out of anxious sleep. In the morning, the nurses had some happier news: they didn't know how she was doing it, but

Francesca was holding on. There was a ray of hope, but it was all too brief. Later that day, doctors struggled to stabilise Francesca's blood pressure, and at six o'clock that evening, one of the chief consultants called Chris and Maria into his office. His words were blunt, direct, but after months of inconclusiveness and ambiguity, they were needed.

Maria remembers them well. "He said: 'We can keep trying if you want to, but she is going to die'. I think we needed to hear the words, really, to have someone else say that, rather than to keep on hoping."

Chris and Maria were left with a heartbreaking choice: keep trying on what was almost certainly a fruitless pursuit, or take Francesca off the machines and hold her. They chose the latter; and, held by her parents, Francesca died half an hour later.

The midwives asked whether Chris and Maria wanted to call their family, to provide support and encouragement: they declined. This was a time just for them and their new baby, a time to spend together.

Chris was grieving, of course, but distracted himself by carrying out tasks and supporting his family. "He phoned round everybody," recalls Maria, lovingly. "How he did that, I don't know. He went out into the car park, phoned his mum, and spoke to the kids."

Francesca died on November 11th, 2009. Although Maria could have returned home the same day, she waited until the following Saturday. "I didn't want to go home and face it all," she says. "Just to walk out of hospital without a baby, and you're passing men coming in with baby seats to take their baby home… even though we had the problems all along, we still didn't actually think that was going to happen."

Beau, five years old at the time, was asleep when Chris rang with the awful news. He knew that he had a new baby sister, and so when Chris picked him up from school the next day he was eager to find out more. He asked what Francesca's hair was like, and then cried when Chris told him the terrible news.

For the most part, Chris and Maria's families left them to grieve, but friends talked to them – something they craved. "Nobody knows what to do," says Maria.

Friends were wonderful; lesser-known acquaintances tried their hardest to be helpful, but many failed miserably. Not knowing what to say, they ended up stumbling over their words, as Maria recollects: "They ask 'Have you had the baby?', and then are horrified when you tell them the news," she says. "Then they ask 'How many children have you got?'. When I say 'three', they react as if to say 'Well, what do you want more for?'"

For the first couple of weeks Chris and Maria spent most of their time crying; Maria would be watching the television, and feel the tears suddenly come. A clinical psychologist helped her deal with her emotions, and over time they both learned to cope with the terrible grief that losing a child brings. They became closer; not just as a couple, but as a family. Grief can be a very galvanising experience. "Chris was brilliant," Maria smiles. "Some men aren't so sensitive, but I couldn't have done it without him."

Both Chris and Maria had to continue being parents to their three children, as well as trying to grieve; a feat made all the more difficult by the fact it was the Christmas period. "That was the hardest thing, those first few months at Christmas time," recalls Maria, "seeing pink bundles in carry cots everywhere. It was really hard. You're faced with Christmas, you've got other kids; you've got to carry on for them."

*

On Francesca's first birthday, her brothers and sister released balloons in her memory. By then, Maria and Chris were once again expecting a new arrival. "Almost while we were still holding Francesca, we both said we'd try again," remembers Maria. "From my point of view, I had to have that to hold on to, otherwise it would have been harder to cope."

By a strange quirk of fate, Maria fell pregnant with Roxanna in March; the same month in which she had the news that she was expecting Francesca. Friends and family reacted in horror and disbelief, but Chris and Maria felt quite differently. "When you've lost one, people don't understand how you feel," explains Maria, "but the desperation to have one then is even stronger, because you were going to have one but it's been taken away."

It had been a difficult couple of years for Chris and Maria: the horrible childbirth experience with Beau, then the loss of Francesca. Then, in early 2010, Beau was diagnosed with Type 1 Diabetes. The news came as a total shock, and was only discovered when Beau suddenly fell seriously ill. "It was touch and go for a while," recalls Maria. "My legs just went from beneath me. I had noticed he was drinking a lot, I suppose, and he had started wetting the bed, but you don't think your five-year-old is a diabetic."

This, coupled with the terrible experiences of previous pregnancies, meant that neither Chris nor Maria could relax as they awaited Roxanna's arrival. At the twelve-week scan, Maria's heart was pounding. They had an appointment at a private practice where the staff were aware of her loss, and were very prompt in reassuring her that all was well. The same could not be said, unfortunately, for the hospital staff.

"A week after I lost Francesca I had the doctor phoning me up, saying 'How is the baby?'" recalls Maria. "I didn't know what to say. Chris got very angry about it."

Thankfully, Roxanna's nine months in the womb passed without incident; Maria providing such a comfortable home that she had to be induced on 1st January, 2011. At 2.24 the next morning, Roxanna was born:

Both Chris and Maria were anxious to hear one simple sound; a sound hated by many parents, but which was now craved. "We were waiting to hear that cry. When it came, it was such a relief."

Roxanna had arrived, and both she and mum were fit and healthy. At five months old, she is alert, lively, full of smiles and adored by a proud mother and father. But the memories of Francesca will never fade, and occasionally her siblings will ask about her.

In Britain especially, it is all too easy for those who suffer a loss to maintain a stiff upper lip and bottle emotions up inside. Maria urges parents who find themselves in a similar situation to talk about their feelings and experiences, to vent at anyone who is willing to listen – and, above all, to remember that time is the greatest healer. "People need to know that you can go on and have another baby after something awful happens."

Fifteen minutes into the interview, Chris' phone rings: it's the local youth club. Nathan has fallen off his bike, and is on his way to casualty with a suspected fractured wrist. "That's all we need," sighs Maria, as Chris excuses himself and heads down to the hospital. Yet another hurdle to leap in what has been a draining and tragic few years for the Riley household; but one which, like all others before, will be overcome as a family.

Baby Number Two

Louise cringes every time she mentions the nightclub in Leamington Spa where she met her husband, Adam. Describing the dingy room as "hideous" with "sticky carpets", she recalls being stood at the bar one night with her colleagues, waiting for her order: a glass of water.

"All of a sudden I had my arm yanked, and a guy pulled me over," she remembers, with a smile. "It was Adam. He said, 'You look as bored as I am, come and talk to me'."

Talk they did, and even though Adam was – in Louise's words – "as drunk as a skunk", she found his conversation interesting. "I thought: 'If he's able to converse this well when he's drunk, what's he like when he's sober?'" A couple of days later, she called him, and – after finding they had more in common than a mutual dislike of grimy flooring, they were married on the longest day of the year: 21st June, 2008.

Until she met Adam, Louise had been fiercely independent: in her early twenties she lived in America for two years, working as a nanny. It was there she learned the importance of reading to children, a principle she has kept with her to this day: every night she reads three stories to their two-and-a-half year-old son, Arthur, followed by three prayers. His favourite book? *The Gruffalo*, of course; followed closely by *Zog*.

From America, Louise travelled to Australia with her

boyfriend. Unfortunately, it wasn't to be, and they broke up after two months; but Louise stayed for another ten, working as a market researcher. Upon returning to England, she bought a run-down house, which she refurbished with her dad (she fondly refers to herself as a "daddy's girl"), and enjoyed living the single life. "I was smoking lots and drinking lots, and going to Rio's regularly." Cringe.

Soon after they married, and after a smooth pregnancy, Arthur was born – although his timing could have been better. Louise began her maternity leave from work two weeks before her due date, and was looking forward to a fortnight of rest before the big day; but it wasn't to be. "My waters broken at work on the last day I was there."

Fortunately, Louise and Adam had a little time; Arthur arrived naturally two days later, after Louise exercised her rights as a mother and refused to be induced. When the time did come for Arthur's arrival, Louise opted for a water birth. "It seemed a really natural way of doing it," she says. "I did expect to have gas and air, but I was so busy concentrating on my breathing and thinking 'Oh dear, oh dear', that it never came."

Before entering the birthing pool, Louise sought pain relief in the form of a TENS machine – as Adam found out to his disadvantage. Louise's contractions were coming thick and fast, and so even when the TENS machine was on permanent boost she couldn't feel a thing. "We walked round to the pool room, and I had to take it off," she recalls. "Adam unpeeled it, and it virtually shot him across the room! He said 'How did you cope with that?'... I didn't realise it was still going!"

Adam was a great source of encouragement and support during labour, and Louise is sympathetic. "It's quite hard for the guys," she muses. "They can't do a lot, can they? I knew Adam was there, and he was supporting me when I went to the toilet, but I think he felt a bit helpless."

Perhaps that should be *mostly* sympathetic. "At one point, when I was in the pool, I put my head down into the water. My hair was falling over my face, and so Adam wiped it away for me; but then a contraction came, and he was still wiping, so I growled 'Get off!'. It was all I could say. When the pain had gone, I had to say 'I'm sorry, but please don't touch me when I'm having a contraction'."

Eventually, Arthur was born, weighing in at a healthy seven pounds and one ounce. Louise vividly remembers seeing him resting on Adam's chest, and describes it as "a lovely sight".

Louise took twelve months maternity leave, and by the time she returned to work she and Adam had decided to try for another. They were both the youngest of three children, and so it seemed a natural and nicely symmetrical progression for Arthur to be accompanied by another two siblings.

A couple of months after deciding to try for another baby, Louise started showing the symptoms of pregnancy. Besides having tender breasts, her sense of smell went through the roof. "I'd go 'How much gum are you chewing?', or 'Your beer stinks!', and Adam would just look at me as if to say 'Oh yeah, when's your period due?'"

After a couple of negative pregnancy tests – which Louise took little heed of, her instinct telling her otherwise – she waited for a week and took another test. This time, the result came back positive. Both Louise and Adam were thrilled.

Five weeks later, they went to London to watch the cricket and do a bit of sightseeing before going on holiday to St. Ives with her mother-in-law. It was around that time when, unbeknown to Louise, her baby stopped growing. "I felt really off the whole holiday," she recalls, "like I wasn't participating. I was knackered, and spent a lot of time in bed, feeling sick."

Louise and Adam put her illness down to stress: their house was on the market at the time, and many days were spent tidying every room in preparation for numerous viewings. "It was all a bit manic and stressful."

The tension was relieved somewhat when Adam threw Louise a surprise fortieth birthday party. She took the chance to tell her friends and family the news that she and Adam were expecting their second child. "Pretty much all my friends and family were at the party, and when I did a little speech I said: 'And, for those who don't know… '. That was one Sunday afternoon. The following Sunday, I started bleeding."

The bleeding began at six o'clock in the morning. Louise rang NHS Direct, who advised that she needed to see a doctor at her local surgery, which opened an hour later. After sixty minutes, which Louise describes as "horrible", she rang the receptionist, who informed her that she would speak to a doctor as soon as possible and ring her back.

Finally, at 11.30am, Louise received a call from her doctor, who said that they had organised an appointment for her to see a midwife at the local hospital. The appointment was in two days time.

"It was just hideous," recalls Louise. "If they had said to me, 'If you've started bleeding, there's probably very little anyone can do about it, we suggest you rest', I'd know where I stood. But they left me in limbo for two days. I was panicking, and thinking 'What's happening?'"

22

Adam tried his best to remain positive, but the maternal instinct Louise trusted so much told her otherwise. "I knew it wasn't going to happen," she remembers, sadly. "I'm a bit more of a realist, I think. You know your own body, and you know when it's not right."

Did she know much about the risks that come with pregnancy? "Nothing. I knew nothing about miscarriages at all. None of my friends had discussed it with me. You hear things in the news, but I'd just had a healthy baby boy, everything went OK, and you just assume it's going to be the same."

The appointment came, and Louise sat in the waiting room of the ultrasound department, surrounded by mothers carrying live babies and with the train track sound of heartbeats coming through the wall from the adjacent sonography room. Adam continued to be supportive, but Louise was, in her words, "Crying my eyes out, thinking 'This isn't happening'. I can hear the heartbeats of other babies, and all I can think is 'When they do that to mine, it's not going to be there'."

They spoke to the early pregnancy midwife, and went in for a scan. The sonographer confirmed Louise and Adam's worst fears – but, in the face of such grief, Louise found a strange sense of reassurance. "As soon as I heard the scan and heard that the baby was the size of a five week-old, this tiny little bean, I knew that it wasn't the size it should be. I'm a woman of the world, I've been around a long time, so I know if it's not meant to be, it's not meant to be."

Louise believes in God, and her faith helped her to recognise that everything happens for a reason. Knowing that her baby had stopped growing allowed her to rationalise what had happened and helped her make sense of what lay ahead. But it's the fact that she had to wait so long to be seen which continues to be the cause of much frustration.

"If I'd had that scan two days earlier it would have been so much better to deal with mentally," she argues. "Those two days were torture, almost. As soon as I saw the scan… what I then had to go through was still pretty hideous, but it made a lot more sense to me."

Compounding Louise's frustration was the fact that she was made to wait alongside mothers with healthy babies. "I was just stunned that we had to go into the same little waiting area, and that I had to wait so long to get there," she says. "A quarter of all pregnancies end in miscarriage. Hospitals have got to make facility for that."

Louise and Adam made the choice to let nature take its course, feeling that the next few days would provide the chance to mourn and grieve that they were unsure would be obtained if there had been a form of clinical removal. Although she was physically fit to return to work within a few days, Louise took two weeks off to allow herself time to regain a semblance of emotional fitness – although she still believes she went back to work too early.

Her colleagues were all very sympathetic, and being back in the office allowed Louise the chance to settle back into a routine – and, with it, achieve a sense of normality. "I always think you go to work to escape your problems at home," she theorises, "and you come home to escape your problems at work."

Adam, forever supportive, was her strength in the heart-wrenching few days which followed their loss. "He was upset," she remembers, "but he was trying to be strong for me. He was saying, 'This is hard for me emotionally, so I know it's hard for you, and you're going through the physical side of it as well'. He was very supportive, and so were my parents."

*

Louise and Adam wanted to try for another child straight away, but were advised by the midwife to wait for a few months to help them recover emotionally from their loss. Then, one Sunday morning, as Adam was having a lie-in, Louise took a pregnancy test. The result was positive. At the same time, Arthur toddled into the bathroom.

Louise recalls how she broke the news to Adam. "I cleaned the test off, gave it to Arthur, and said 'Go and give that to Daddy'. Daddy looks, and he doesn't know what it means, even though it clearly says on the test what means pregnant and what doesn't. He's like, 'What's that... is that right?'"

It was right; and both Louise and Adam were delighted, but it was a joy tempered by past experience. "We really wanted another one, but you know when you've been hurt you close ranks a bit, you don't want to be hurt again."

Whilst during her pregnancy with Arthur the risk of something going wrong didn't even cross Louise's mind, she now assumed the worst would happen once again. "Losing a baby changed our expectations and outlook for this pregnancy," she explains. "It's affected me a lot. Yesterday's scan, our twenty-week one, was actually the first time I'd got excited about this pregnancy."

Their caution is evident: despite being five months pregnant, only Louise and Adam's parents currently know, along with a handful of close friends. This time, they are a lot more mindful

25

of the risks that pregnancy brings, as Louise attests: "You don't look for the negative, but once you know it's there, you can't help but take it into consideration. I've been a lot more aware of lifting things, and so on. My symptoms now are similar to those I had with Arthur. Looking back at the baby I miscarried, the symptoms were different – and then stopped."

At twenty weeks, Louise is glowing, and progressing well: but this pregnancy has not been without its dramas. The day after taking Arthur to Thomas Land at Drayton Manor, she felt a sharp pain in her hip. Convinced it wasn't pregnancy-related, she made an appointment to see her GP; who told her that she could feel a hernia. After spending two days flat on her back with her knees bent on doctor's orders, the pain still hadn't subsided – so Louse returned to the doctor, this time to be told that there was no hernia, but that instead she wanted to listen to the baby's heart. And so, she prodded and poked using a Doppler scanner: and couldn't find a heartbeat.

"I thought: 'stupid cow'," recalls Louise. "I knew it wasn't anything to do with my pregnancy."

She was sent for a scan at the same hospital in which she had given birth to Arthur and had confirmation that her second child had been lost. It was only when her appointment was with the same early pregnancy midwife, who had informed them of their loss, that Louise started worrying. Fortunately, a heartbeat was swiftly found, and both Louise and Adam could concentrate on the rest of the pregnancy.

Their little baby is due in mid-October, 2011. Convinced she was having another boy, as her symptoms were identical to those she experienced when expecting Arthur, Louise was overjoyed to discover that she is carrying a girl.

Does she have any names in mind? "Charlotte Elizabeth," she says, without hesitation. "I've thought about it for so many years. I've never thought of a big white wedding or anything like that, but I have thought about Charlotte Elizabeth."

Adam, too, is delighted at the prospect of a daughter. By a charming coincidence, the spare room is already painted pink, and so the reduced amount of DIY only adds to his joy. "He's really pleased we're having a girl," grins Louise. "She's going to be 'Daddy's little girl'. It'll be hell when she brings her first boyfriend home. He'll be a strict daddy, I think."

Arthur cannot wait to meet his little sister; but, at such a tender age, sometimes struggles to grasp the situation. "He doesn't properly understand at all," laughs Louise. "This morning, on the way to nursery, he finished his juice and said 'Juice have a baby?' He still has a lot to learn!"

Whilst her loss has not had a profound effect on Louise's outlook on life – "I think having Arthur changed my priorities completely," she says – she will never forget. And she hopes that, through her experiences, she can help others in a similar situation. "I hope nothing like this happens to any of my friends, but I hope they know that if it does, they can come to me, and I can help. I wish I'd had a friend I knew who'd gone through it. I'm all for speaking out about it."

So, finally, with a son already growing up fast and the imminent arrival of a daughter, is Louise still planning on having a third?

"We'll see," she says, with a chuckle.

Footprints in the Sand

by Mary Stevenson

and a source of great comfort to Louise and Adam

One night I had a dream.
I dreamed I was walking along the beach with the Lord
and across the sky flashed scenes from my life.
For each scene I noticed two sets of footprints,
one belonged to me and the other to the Lord.

When the last scene of my life flashed before me,
I looked back at the footprints in the sand.
I noticed that many times along the path of my life,
there was only one set of footprints.
I also noticed that it happened at the very lowest
and saddest times in my life.

This really bothered me and I questioned the Lord about it.
"Lord, you said that once I decided to follow you,
you would walk with me all the way,
but I have noticed that during the most troublesome times in
my life
there is only one set of footprints.
"I don't understand why in times when I needed you most,
you should leave me."

The Lord replied, "My precious, precious child,
I love you and I would never, never leave you
during your times of trial and suffering.
"When you saw only one set of footprints,
it was then that I carried you."

Leo

As far as love stories go, Marianne and Nathan's is very much a 21st century tale. Their eyes did not meet across a smoky room, nor did they fall in love on the dance floor of a friend's wedding. Instead, Marianne received an email from Nathan through a dating website; and, after a few dates – including a trip to Cheddar Gorge ("which was good, even though he made me climb up Jacob's Ladder") – Nathan got down on bended knee on Bonfire Night and proposed.

The wedding was held on a beautifully sunny day in the village church where Marianne grew up, with the reception afterwards being reached by car. "There are a few things I would have changed," muses Marianne – a sentiment perhaps shared by many married women – "but it was so perfect, even though it was very rushed to get ready."

When Marianne fell pregnant with their first baby, it was a happy surprise: but her mother's intuition told her that something wasn't right – and, early on in the pregnancy, she suffered from bleeding and stomach cramps. Being their first child, with the excitement it brings, they had already told friends and family by the time a scan confirmed that the baby had been lost. "I just felt numb, and so sad."

Both Marianne and Nathan knew that pregnancy brought risks, but they were unaware just how common miscarriage is.

Classed as the loss of a foetus before the twenty-fourth week of gestation, miscarriage in the UK occurs in around one in four pregnancies. "I remember speaking to the midwife a week before," says Marianne, "and she was talking about all the tests you could have, and things which I knew about."

But there was no mention of miscarriage, and how much of a threat it is. What would Marianne do, if she had the power, to increase the awareness of miscarriage? "More scans, better care, more midwives – and more media attention, so it's not such a taboo subject. I want the media to get it right, and be more sensitive over it."

Losing a baby made Marianne and Nathan more convinced to try for another, but they were told by health professionals to wait for a few months to allow her body to recover from the physical trauma of a miscarriage. It was around six months later when the blue lines showed that Marianne was pregnant.

"I felt really pleased, but very scared," recalls Marianne. "I was on tenterhooks; I didn't want it to end like it did before."

The pregnancy itself was, in Marianne's words, "Not enjoyable". A test showed up positive for gestational diabetes, and Marianne was told to regularly see a consultant – whose bedside manner was sadly lacking. "He was very rude about me, as I am a larger lady, and so because I was large I was going to have a big baby," remembers Marianne, with disdain. "I hated going."

The constant stream of information from health workers – albeit important – made Marianne feel like "a school kid again". "I had to see a dietician," she recalls. "I knew what foods to eat, and what not to eat. I felt very small."

At thirty-two weeks, in the summer heatwave of 2006, Marianne went into premature labour. This came as a surprise, of course, and she found herself in hospital without a change of clothes or her maternity book. After three days of close monitoring – and a steroid injection – she was allowed home. However, five weeks later, her blood pressure rose and she had protein in her urine; and so, after another spell in hospital, she was sent home and closely monitored at a different hospital closer to where Marianne and Nathan lived.

The Friday following her referral to Weston, Marianne had a scan. "I remember listening to the midwife: she said that this baby wouldn't be much longer. On the Saturday morning I went into labour!"

It was 11.30am, in fact, when Marianne first thought her waters had gone. Her father and sister-in-law had come over for cream cakes, but not even a family visit could dull the unbearable pain that she was feeling. "Nathan drove us to hospital, and we got there about 2pm," she remembers. "I was checked over by a young midwife. She said that my waters hadn't broken, and that I was two centimetres dilated, but to go home as it wasn't worth waiting around."

Thus followed a rather bizarre couple of hours. Back at home, the only place Marianne felt vaguely comfortable was on the toilet. "I was in agony, wondering when the pain would pass."

Having had previous experience of hospital food – "It wasn't great", she recalls – Marianne instead ate food fresh from McDonalds to give her the energy she needed for the next few hours. The pain did not subside, and a phone call to the hospital was met with the advice to take paracetamol and have a bath.

"They were trying to fob me off," states Marianne. "I could hardly get in the bath! I could no longer take the pain; Nathan rang the hospital back, and we went in."

When they reached the hospital, they were met by the same young midwife who had sent them home a few hours earlier. After an assessment, she apologised: Marianne was fully dilated, her waters had broken, and baby Gracie was moments away from being born.

There was a problem, though: Gracie's back was aligned with Marianne's, and she was only just beginning to turn. The need to push was diminishing, and so an exhausted Marianne was put on a hormone drip. A doctor came to see her, and examinations revealed that Gracie was stuck on her mum's pelvis. A forceps delivery was required.

Nathan was told to don a pair of scrubs and a face mask – clothes which Marianne refers to as "his George Clooney outfit" – and she was wheeled into theatre. It was "pretty scary stuff", recalls Marianne, recalling that she had to tell the anaesthetist every time she was having a contraction in case the spinal tap he was inserting was jolted and she was paralysed.

All went well, though, and Gracie was delivered by forceps at 12.19am on 16th July, 2006. Slightly jaundiced, she spent two days in hospital in a heated ventilator, away from the windows, in the middle of a heatwave. "Silly, we both thought."

As an infant, Gracie has always wanted to make friends: "She always used to go and hug other children if she sees them in the playground!" A redhead, or "strawberry blonde", as Marianne calls it, Gracie has a temper, but has a great sense of humour. "A very loving and caring child," recalls Marianne fondly, "but she can be very stubborn at times!"

*

It was two years before Marianne and Nathan once again found out that they were expecting another baby. They were both thrilled, but disappointed by the care they received from the community midwife. "She was rubbish," recalls Marianne. "It was like she didn't really know me. She always asked for the results of tests a long time after they were carried out. I felt I was kind of left to get on with my pregnancy."

The pregnancy itself went well until around thirty-nine weeks, when Marianne went to hospital experiencing strong Braxton Hicks contractions. She was given medication, and also tested for Group B Streptococcus, carried by a quarter of women who are of childbearing age, and the most common cause of bacterial infection in newborn babies. The results came back negative a few weeks later, but by this time Marianne was concerned about the latest development in what was proving to be a worrisome few days: her milk had come in early.

She phoned the maternity ward, who advised her that although it wasn't a normal occurrence, it certainly wasn't anything to worry about. They didn't ask her to go into hospital to be checked over, though, nor did the community midwife offer to make a home visit when Marianne called her to discuss her concerns.

At forty-one weeks, Marianne was booked in for a stretch and sweep, something the midwife assumed she was aware of. "Hardly!" exclaims Marianne. Thanks to a "stinking cold", Marianne cancelled the appointment, but was not offered a home visit. She said no more of it at the time: but couldn't shake the feeling that something was wrong with her baby. The maternal instincts which had proven to be so accurate during her first pregnancy had returned.

A few days later, strong contractions woke her from an afternoon nap. They were ten minutes apart, and were getting worse. After a while, though, they subsided, and Marianne walked down the street to where her mother-in-law lived for some tea. Nathan came home from work, by which point the contractions had returned. Anticipating the imminent childbirth, Nathan rushed back to his apartment to fetch the overnight bags. "It felt like they had been gone ages," recalls Marianne, who had lost her mucous plug by this time. "I was in lots of pain and couldn't move, so my mother-in-law rang for an ambulance."

An ambulance car was first to arrive, and the paramedics provided Marianne with gas and air as they waited for the ambulance. "I remember feeling really embarrassed, thinking 'Why did she call them?'" she recollects. "I wasn't to know I actually wouldn't make it to hospital to deliver my little boy, Leo."

The ambulance sped towards the hospital, Marianne's family following close behind. The ride was very bumpy, which caused Marianne a lot of pain and discomfort. Her pain grew stronger. "They blue-lit me, but then I felt like I needed to push, so the ambulance pulled over in a lay-by at Leigh Woods."

Two pushes, and Leo was born. "I never heard him cry, and I didn't see my son," recalls Marianne. "He wasn't breathing. They tried to resuscitate, they worked on him, they thought he perhaps had lots of mucous on his chest. Nathan tried to say it was alright. I think I knew."

Another ambulance came. Marianne caught only a thirty-second glimpse of her son before he was whisked away to hospital. She arrived soon afterwards: "I remember seeing my mother and sister-in-law. I just kept my head down; I didn't want to look up."

Nathan had left the room to call Marianne's parents and

update them on what had unfolded. It was at that point that the doctor entered the room in which Marianne was placed to deliver the placenta.

"I remember telling the doctor: 'Please wait, my husband is out of the room.' It was confirmed Leo was an angel. He had never breathed, he had never cried; he had gone to heaven. I swear I had felt him move – it must have been the placenta."

Leo had been dead for a day or so; his skin had started to peel. "It was the worst day of my life."

Marianne held Leo as she was wheeled to the Lavender Suite, a room dedicated by Sands for newly bereaved parents. "I felt shocked," she recalls. "My Leo had grown his wings; I couldn't let anyone else see that he was dead. They were having breathing babies, but I hadn't."

The doctor, plagued by other emergencies, could only make fleeting visits. The midwife "popped in and out". There was no dedicated bereavement midwife, and Marianne was left for most of the night. "I wish someone was there to give me guidance," she says. She also wishes that she had requested a post mortem, but knew that there was a high possibility that the results would come back inconclusive. Her placenta was tested; all was clear.

Marianne had some photographs taken of Leo. These, and his scan photos, remain her most treasured memories of her son. The funeral was held at the same church in which she had been married, and where Gracie was baptised. "My sister had written a poem. We had a CD of 'Twinkle Twinkle Little Star' playing as we left: that's what Gracie always sang to her brother when he was in my tummy."

The next few weeks went by in a blur. Marianne's appetite was barely there, and at times she felt like she wanted to run away, but Gracie provided the strength to deal with her darkest days as a family. Their pain was exacerbated by new neighbours, who had two young children.

"They talked to their kids like rubbish," remembers Marianne angrily, "and they had a little boy of about one. I just remember hearing him cry. I yearned to hear Leo cry."

Like many parents, Marianne started to blame herself. Why didn't she know Leo had stopped moving? Why hadn't she acted on her intuition? She and Nathan had argued a day or so prior to Leo being born: did that have something to do with it?

Nathan was also struggling to cope with his loss. "He became very depressed, and was suicidal at one point. I couldn't understand why he was blaming himself; I felt I was the one to blame. He had tablets and some counselling from the NHS. I tried to get on with life for the sake of Gracie, and found it really helpful chatting to people on the Sands forums, whereas Nathan shut his pain in more."

It was Nathan's role to tell friends and family the awful news and make arrangements for the funeral. "I couldn't cope with talking to people on the phone," says Marianne. "I would only be able to text or speak online; Nathan was the one keeping me going."

That's not to say Marianne didn't *want* to talk to people; but she found that some asked too many questions, and her work colleagues felt so uncomfortable that Marianne ended up being pushed away. As a result, she lost touch with many friends; but her relationship with Nathan was strengthened hugely. "We talked more."

A few days after Leo's funeral, Marianne, Nathan and Gracie felt they had to get away, where no-one knew of their loss. They went to Devon, and stayed in a forest lodge for a few days.

"Leo brought us snow," remembers Marianne fondly, "a present for Gracie. She loved playing in it, building a snowman and a snow owl. We had a lovely time there."

Unfortunately, hospital staff continued to be lacking in support for the grieving couple. Marianne describes her local doctors as a "disgrace", noting that it took weeks for someone from the surgery to get in touch. She made a complaint to the hospital about the lack of care received – not just by the family, but by Leo himself. A sample of skin was taken from his thigh for use in a genetics test, and as a result, he had bled all over his outfit; meaning Marianne and Nathan were unable to see their boy for a day until the funeral directors dressed Leo in clean clothes. A consultant referred to Leo as 'a foetus'; whilst waiting for one of the consultant's appointments, Marianne was asked if she was there for a twenty-week scan. Eventually, the Head of Midwifery visited them to discuss the matter.

Four simple words encouraged and supported Marianne and Nathan during this terrible time: *it's not your fault*. Gradually, they stopped blaming themselves. Marianne eventually found a local baby loss support group, and found that talking about her loss in the knowledge that other people understood her pain was a great help. "We all helped each other with our grief," she says. "The lady who ran the group was very sensitive and warming."

*

A year to the day after Leo died, Samuel was born. "I had planned to be induced on 10th February, but Samuel had other ideas and came at thirty-five weeks. I think he had waited for Leo to have his second birthday."

Marianne and Nathan experienced a "mixed bag of emotions" when they discovered they were pregnant with Samuel. Initially, they told only immediate family, who were happy but shied away from talking about it. "It might have been my fault," admits Marianne. "I wasn't so jolly this time."

As with her previous pregnancies, Marianne endured a range of tests whilst she was pregnant, as well as being told by a locum consultant to go to hospital immediately if she was concerned about the baby's movements. Sound advice, but perhaps it could have been delivered better. "He really scared the life out of me. My husband spoke with my consultant, and we arranged to be scanned by her from then on. I felt I was going through enough."

After Marianne endured five hours in labour, and after a lot of pushing ("the slow part was getting the back and hind quarters out"), Samuel was born, weighing a healthy 7lb 5oz. The labour was brief but demanding, and Marianne required stitches. "That was the most painful thing," she recalls, "and I just sucked so hard on the gas and air at one point that I thought I had gone to heaven with Leo. I was so relieved when it was over with. I wish that someone had intervened and given me stronger drugs."

Marianne and Nathan's experience has changed their outlook on life. "Live for today," says Marianne. "My children are so precious." She often talks of Leo, not least because she worries that friends and family may have forgotten him. Gracie hasn't, though, and talks often of him.

Every year, on Leo's birthday, Marianne and her family have a cake and release balloons. Then, in the evening, at 9.15 – the same time he was born – they release lanterns and light candles in his memory. And, now and again, Leo brings some more snow, as a present for his big sister.

A Letter to Leo

Leo, I miss you with all my heart.

I think of you every day, as does your big sister Gracie and your little brother Samuel. I hope you are having fun with all your angel friends.

Love you always, son.

Love,

Mummy, Daddy, Gracie and Samuel
Xxxxxx

Jack

Claire Rhoades and her husband, Marc, had always said that if scans showed that their baby had any abnormalities or conditions they would continue with the pregnancy. Having worked as a Teaching Assistant at a special school for almost two decades, Claire was well experienced in looking after children who needed a little more care and attention; which is why they viewed the twenty-week scan – often known as the 'abnormality scan' as simply an extra scan, a bonus.

They never imagined anything would crop up. "They do say it takes a bit longer, because it's more detailed," says Claire, "but we just got a gut feeling that something wasn't right."

The sonographer left the room to fetch a consultant, who conducted a scan and told the worried parents that he was concerned about the measurements of the nuchal fold, behind the neck of the baby. Claire instinctively knew that this meant her baby had a high risk of suffering from Down's Syndrome. They were referred to a local hospital and waited for two weeks to receive a scan appointment date: the "longest two weeks ever", as Claire recalls.

During the agonising wait, Claire and Marc once again discussed how they felt about the possibility of raising a child with special needs; and, once again, they decided they were happy to continue with the pregnancy. The worst thing that could be diagnosed, they thought, was Down's Syndrome: which, to the expectant parents, was "not a huge issue".

Finally, the appointment came and the scan was conducted. Claire and Marc had been warned beforehand that they should not expect much talking, that the sonographer would be taking time to carefully inspect and analyse their baby. After what seemed like an age, the scan finished and the concerned parents were placed in a small side room. After a while, a consultant entered. Claire describes him as "horrific".

"He basically just came in and said 'Right, you're not carrying any fluid, and your baby's got no stomach and no bladder. I can do a termination, I can do it today. If you want to think about it I can pop out."

He left the room, leaving Claire and Marc reeling at the devastating news they had just been given so bluntly. Through a pane of glass in the door, Claire could see the consultant standing in the corridor. "He was laughing and joking," she remembers, angered at the thought. "It's just part of his job, isn't it, but he'd turned our world completely upside down. We just sat there; we didn't know what to do."

In the end, they decided to do nothing; not for another fortnight, at least. They needed time to come to terms with what they had been told. They informed the consultant of their decision. "He said: 'Well, you can do, but it's not going to make a blind bit of difference."

Back at home, the reality of the consultant's lack of feeling hit home, and the stunned parents demanded another appointment with a different consultant. The appointment came, and they were seen by a professor. Fortunately, he was quite unlike his colleague – "lovely", in fact – and he carried out a scan which

42

amazed them all. It transpired that Jack did have a stomach, and he did have a bladder. The nuchal fold was still a concern, true, but all of his organs were present and correct. The relief was immense, tinged with anger at the ineptitude of the previous consultant.

"How many people would have a termination after being told that news?" asks Marc. "When we were there, there were loads of young girls in the waiting room. They'd have gotten rid of their baby straight away."

The news was not all good, however. Claire was carrying barely any amniotic fluid, and as a result her baby's lungs were struggling to mature. Although Claire had only been pregnant for around six months at this point, her birth plan had now been decided: at thirty-two weeks she would have a Caesarean section, with the incision running from her sternum to her navel, instead of across the base of her abdomen. This would allow more space for her baby to be removed, as the lack of fluid meant even the lightest touch would cause bruising.

In an attempt to develop her baby's lungs, Claire had steroid injections every Thursday; after which, without fail, one cheek would be glowing the next day – a "very bizarre" side-effect. Then, two weeks later, she began leaking fluid, and rushed to hospital. The doctors carried out an inspection, and told Claire that she wasn't holding her bladder, even doing a swab to prove it. This happened on a few occasions, and each time Claire was insistent that the leak was the small amount of amniotic fluid that she was carrying. Each time, she was told that she was mistaken.

"They made us feel like 'Oh, here they are again'," remembers Marc, "new parents, overreacting."

One morning, at twenty-eight weeks, Claire went into work.

A colleague asked how she was. "I said, 'I just don't feel right this morning, I feel all niggly'." As the day progressed, Claire felt worse. She had what she describes as "period pains", and eventually a friend drove her home. Claire went to bed. The pains kept coming, though, so she phoned a friend.

"I said, 'You know when you're in labour, what do the pains feel like? I feel like I've got period pains, and they're coming every ten minutes.' My friend just replied: 'I think you'd better phone Marc.'"

Claire rang Marc, as well as the hospital, who told them to come in to get checked out. When they arrived, they were met by the same doctor who had examined Claire when she was losing fluid. This time, Claire would not be sent home: she was six centimetres dilated.

The hospital had no facilities for delivering premature babies, so Claire was sent to the another hospital by ambulance, as Marc went on ahead. It was a hospital which Claire had always said that she didn't want to give birth in; her cousin had died there of leukaemia at just sixteen years of age, and the building held awful memories. But, at the time, this was the last concern on her mind.

"They thought I was going to have him in the car park," she recalls. "Everything was such a blur. We thought we were just going to be sent home; we hadn't got anything with us. I was more upset that we'd packed a bag, and it was at home!"

They were put into a side ward, and given a midwife who gave Claire's thick file of notes a cursory glance whilst the worried parents "hadn't got a clue what was going on." Marc asked the midwife how long Claire's discomfort would last. The response he got – "How long is a piece of string?" – was, he feels, particularly insensitive. What was apparent, however, was that it was too late to have the planned Caesarean section.

Claire had never given much thought to a birth plan, as she and Marc had always assumed that the Caesarean would be provided at thirty-two weeks; but she was resolute that she did not want an epidural. In the end, as her contractions worsened and her pain increased, she was given Pethidine. After Jack's birth, Claire and Marc carried out some research on the guidelines for administering this drug, and found that it should never be given if the baby is anticipated to arrive within an hour or two, as it crosses the placenta and will have maximum effect the baby once it arrives. Twenty minutes after Claire was given the Pethidine, Jack was born.

Claire remembers the events immediately before Jack's birth well. "I kept saying to Marc, 'I need to push.' The midwife was at the back of the room, and Marc told her. She said: 'Oh, no, that'll just be the pressure of her water.' I kept saying "I haven't got any water, that's the whole problem!'"

The midwife sauntered out of the room. Marc looked down, and Jack's head was crowning. Bursting into the corridor, he called the midwife back in.

"It was panic stations," he remembers. "She was panicking, pulling the alarm bell, and everyone came running in. Within twenty minutes or so, Jack was born."

Jack was immediately taken away by the hospital staff, who didn't tell the exhausted and confused parents where they were going. "We didn't know anything. Jack gave a little cry, which we were amazed at, and they just took him off."

To add to the new parents' problems, the Pethidine was taking its toll on Claire, who was vomiting continuously. Marc was passing her cardboard bowls, and she was filling them up one by one, and being sick on the sheets and down her clothes. Again, the midwife was at the back of the room.

"Marc asked her: 'What shall I do with all this?'" remembers Claire. "She didn't even come over. She was just horrendous, absolutely horrendous."

Eventually, at just after 6pm, they were taken to an upstairs room specifically designated for couples whose babies were suffering from serious conditions. After four hours of working on Jack, a doctor came to see them and told them that their baby had been stabilised, and invited them to visit him.

"The neonatal staff were fantastic," Claire recalls, with a nod of agreement from Marc. "I'll never forget when we first went into that room and saw Jack. He was the youngest baby in there – there were six babies, all with wires coming out of them – but he was the biggest. He was 2lb 12oz, and he looked really strapping compared to some of these babies."

Jack was hooked up to a number of machines. The nursing staff told Claire and Marc what each piece of equipment did, and they spent the next few hours watching their son, and looking at the machinery going up and down. Every now and again, though, the machines would drop, bleep, and they would be sent out of the room.

"We kept saying, 'Next time those doors open it's going to be bad news', but the consultant came out and said, 'He's picked up again, he's amazing. He shouldn't be here, but he is.'"

Jack was suffering complications arising from perforated lungs, the result of a risky procedure carried out after he had been delivered. Claire and Marc had known for a long while that inflating their son's lungs was a necessity, and were aware of the risks it brought. Either the lungs would not be inflated enough, or they would be over-inflated and rupture. Jack now had fluids passing around his body which should not be there. The doctors had done all they could, but there was just too much against him. At around four o'clock in the morning, he passed away; the hospital chaplain came and baptised him.

Claire and Marc returned to their room, "emotionally drained and shattered. It was all so new, and had happened so quickly." Marc had the task of calling friends and family to give them the terrible news, after phoning them earlier with what he thought, at the time, was a better outlook.

"When he was born, I heard him cry," explains Marc, "and I thought 'Things could be alright'; and, because nothing was said, I made the phone calls to parents. I think when I phoned them I gave them a bit of hope that everything was going to be OK."

A few hours later, with Jack in special care, he'd rung them again to say that things were actually not going as well as hoped. The next time he phoned, it was all over. "You feel awful for them," Claire says, "because they felt helpless. It was just out of the blue, they weren't expecting that."

Claire and Marc said their heartbreaking goodbyes to their son, and the hospital staff took Jack away to wash him, clothe him and take prints of his hands and feet. At 5am, when Claire and Marc were both asleep, a nurse knocked on the door and asked if they would like to spend some more time with Jack. Claire still wonders whether they made the right choice. "At the time we said 'No', because we'd said all our goodbyes, and we'd have to do it all over again."

The next morning, the chaplain came to see them. When they told him they lived in the town of Rugby, his face lit up. The nearby city of Coventry holds communal graves for babies, whilst

Rugby boasts one of the best baby cemeteries in the country. The ironic thing was that Claire and Marc had lived in the town all their lives, and never known it was there. "You don't know these things, until you have to."

The bereaved parents saw their baby one more time as he lay in the chapel of rest. Parents and in-laws came to see him, and between them they took dozens of photographs. Their bereavement worker, who was hugely comforting and helpful, took some more photographs a couple of days later and sent them through to Claire and Marc.

"They were not nice," recalls Claire. "It just didn't look like Jack. Marc only looked at them once, and he couldn't look at them any more."

Then followed what both Claire and Marc agree was the "worst period of time for us". There was a delay of three weeks between the post-mortem examination and organising the funeral, in which they were just "in limbo". Claire's parents had previously booked a holiday to Portugal, which they were now planning on cancelling. Claire and Marc urged them not to. "'There's nothing you can do', we said," says Claire. "So my parents just said, 'Why don't you come with us?'"

Claire and Marc deliberated over whether to go or not, and ended up booking a last-minute flight. "We just needed to get away, and it helped. It didn't change anything, but it was away from everything."

When they returned, the post-mortem results were back, and had confirmed that Jack's death was due to perforated lungs. He was not suffering from Down's Syndrome. The funeral could now go ahead, and was carried out at the Clover Leaf Memorial Garden, in what would have been Jack's home town. Described by Claire as a "beautiful place," the children's burial ground is kept separate from the main cemetery, and plots are arranged in the shape of a clover: three petals surrounding a circular centre.

"We couldn't wish for anywhere better for Jack," says Claire, affectionately. "It's full of windmills, toys and baby bunnies running everywhere."

The service was attended by a few close friends and family. For the bereaved parents, it provided a bit of closure, but was the beginning of their darkest days. Reality had hit home. The world was continuing to turn, and somehow Claire and Marc had to find a way of returning to normality.

"I had to stay off work for six weeks," recalls Claire, "because you have to if you have a live birth. For me, that was the longest six weeks of my life."

Claire and Marc had returned to an empty house, with a nursery which had been lovingly prepared. Everywhere they looked, there were babies. "Every channel you watched on the television had babies on it, and everywhere you went there were pregnant women. The worst bit was just waking up in the morning; you realise that you're awake, and it all kicks in. That was just awful.

"It was so surreal. When we came out of the hospital after losing Jack, it was just 'life goes on' for everyone else, and I'm thinking 'How can they be over there laughing and joking?', and it was horrible. Our world had been turned upside down, and everybody was getting on with life."

Friends and family rallied around the couple. Claire's mother found it particularly difficult to cope with the news, taking time off work and being prescribed antidepressants. She spent as much time with her daughter as possible.

Claire and Marc were acting strong, and trying to continue with their lives – but, underneath the surface, they were angry and frustrated. Claire is fit and healthy, had taken her Folic Acid whilst pregnant, and is not a big drinker. "Here I was, being told there was something wrong, and having all these steroid injections, and then I'd go into town and see all these young mothers and teenage girls smoking whilst pregnant. You do everything right, and then this happens."

Marc agrees. "You try and do everything in your life the right way," he says. "I came out of the army, we got a house, we got married, and so the next thing to do is have a baby."

Their anger was not only directed at the injustice they had suffered, but also at the hospital staff who had conducted themselves so poorly when Jack was being born. In the end, Claire and Marc made the decision to write a detailed letter of complaint against the midwife who saw to them and the consultant who had been so abrupt in telling them that their child could be terminated the same day if required.

"When he was born, they just scooped him up and ran out of the room with him," explains Marc, clearly frustrated, "and you look back, and think: 'Surely if he was that poorly there should have been some equipment in the room for him'. When you open the door, there are just stairways and corridors. You think, 'Where did they go running to with this little newborn baby that was dying?'"

Their letter was sent, and a response received. It was very apologetic, but accepted no responsibility. "It said how distressed the midwife was that she thought she was coming across as being insensitive, she can't remember saying 'How long is a piece of string?', and she didn't panic, she knew exactly what she was doing."

After much deliberation, Claire and Marc decided not to take it further. "What's the point?" asks Claire. "It would just have caused more distress, and it wasn't going to bring Jack back. For us, though, it did help to write everything down, to vent our anger a bit."

"Besides, it could have been beneficial to someone else," suggests Marc. "Next time, if she's in the same situation, she would perhaps be more aware of her actions. Being first-timers, we were just waiting for someone else to pick us up, and let us know that everything's going to be alright."

In the weeks and months that followed, Claire became obsessed with visiting Jack's grave, going twice a day to sit and talk to him, to just be near him. She worried about vandals causing damage to his plot and headstone. "I couldn't get over the fact that because he was in a public place, I couldn't protect him."

Claire continued to visit Jack's grave twice a day for weeks, and was struck by how quickly plots adjacent to his were filled. Jack was the fourth baby to be buried on the second petal of the clover leaf. Eleven years later, there are just twelve places left, and construction work is beginning on the third petal.

Claire still visits Jack's grave once a week. Sadly, she has never seen anybody visit the plot next to his, but understands that different people grieve in different ways. "People move away, people find it too hard. When we had Jack's funeral, the director said how lovely it was to see so many people, and that we wouldn't believe the number of funerals he does where it's just him and the undertakers who are there."

Marc found himself taking on a dual role in the time which followed the death of his son: whilst grieving, he felt the need to support his wife. "I just wanted to be there for Claire, really," he clarifies. "I went straight to work when we got back from Portugal. As the man, you just take on the role of the person who holds it all together."

Claire agrees. "It's not until you look on it all afterwards that you realise that a lot is on the dad, because they often have to make the phone calls with bad news. Afterwards, Marc was trying to grieve himself, but equally he was trying to be strong to support me, and I think that's really difficult. A lot of friends would ask me how I was, but not ask after Marc."

*

Claire and Marc were ready to be a mum and dad, but lost the chance to watch their son grow up. Three months after Jack died, they tried again – and Claire became pregnant straight away.

Classed as high-risk, Claire was monitored closely. "It was a textbook pregnancy," she recalls, "but you couldn't enjoy it. Everything was a milestone: you had your twelve-week scan, then your twenty-week scan, and then it was getting past the twenty-eight-week mark. The happiness was taken from us, really. It should have been a lovely pregnancy to enjoy, but we didn't. We just wanted the end to come."

"Every day was a bonus," adds Marc. "It was the longest pregnancy ever. You couldn't enjoy any of the appointments or anything; you were just waiting for something to go wrong."

Whilst dulling their excitement at becoming pregnant again, their experiences had made them more aware of the risks that pregnancy holds. "I'm sure if it had been the other way around, if we'd had Holly first and then gone on to have the problems with Jack, we'd have been a lot wiser."

52

Claire went into labour with Holly two and a half weeks early. They were visiting their local pub when the period-like pains first began, and she spent most of her time walking around the garden. When the contractions were six minutes apart, Marc took her to hospital. At 8pm, almost a year to the day after Jack was born, Holly made her arrival. "It was so quick I didn't have any pain relief," smiles Claire. "It was fantastic."

The first thing the new family did upon leaving the hospital was visit Jack's grave. "I was so desperate to visit him," says Claire, "but it was completely the wrong thing to do; it was just so emotional."

Three years later, Claire and Marc tried once again to fall pregnant, and again they succeeded straight away. However, when Claire was eleven weeks pregnant, she suffered a miscarriage: the first of three, which came in quick succession. "It completely threw us," says Claire. "With having Holly, we were put in a false sense of security. Now, after having a miscarriage, we became obsessed with trying again."

Claire went on to become pregnant, but began to bleed at nine weeks, the baby coming away naturally. Sending Marc out at "stupid-o'clock" to buy pregnancy tests, they tried again, and fell pregnant again. However, once more, Claire suffered a miscarriage; this time, at six weeks.

Claire and Marc were frustrated. They felt they'd had their fair share of bad luck in losing Jack, and now they had to suffer the grief of three miscarriages in a row. Once again, they became pregnant; but, this time – and by "some fluke" – there was no miscarriage.

Although still apprehensive, Claire and Marc could enjoy this pregnancy more than they did when they were expecting Holly.

This time, with their daughter being three years old, they could involve her in appointments and scans, which made it "a bit more enjoyable."

The pregnancy itself went well, until the last month. Doctors and consultants were becoming concerned that her baby was not growing as quickly as they would have liked, and so Claire was booked in for a Caesarean section. However, at thirty-seven weeks, Claire went to the hospital for a routine check-up. The doctor gave her a sweep and – to their surprise – caused Claire to go into labour.

Claire was closely monitored, and as such was unable to move about. As a swarm of trainee doctors and nurses – all fascinated by Claire's pregnancy history – buzzed around the delivery suite, she suffered from excruciating labour pains. The midwife attached a monitor to her baby's head as he still lay in the womb. "That was just so painful," recalls Claire. "I'll never forget that."

Using only gas and air for pain relief, Claire continued through labour. Her midwife was brilliant. "At one point she took the gas and air off me and said: 'For goodness' sake, you've done the hard bit, now sit up and get him out yourself!'"

Claire followed her instructions, and gave birth to a baby boy, Harvey. She and Marc were in shock, but also delighted that they had proven wrong those who had suggested Claire was unable to carry boys. "It was our dream come true, to have a girl and a boy," grins Claire. "It was just fantastic."

Both Holly and Harvey have grown up knowing about their older brother, and he has always been a big part of their lives. Every birthday they tie banners to his headstone, make a cake, and sing 'Happy Birthday'. In 2010, when Jack would have been ten years old, they had a plaque made, which reads: 'Happy 10th

Birthday, from Holly and Harvey'. Last Father's Day, Marc received two cards: one was signed from Holly, and the other from Harvey and Jack. Whenever they go on holiday as a family, they will bring back stones and shells from the beach to decorate his grave.

Harvey went through a phase of making strangers feel very uncomfortable when talking about Jack. Claire laughs. "He'd say: 'I've got a brother and a sister', and they'd say 'No, you've only got a sister'. And he'd respond: 'No, I've got a big brother Jack. He's an angel.' Some people would want to ask more, but most would squirm!"

Claire has found that, when once she received comfort and encouragement from other bereaved parents at the cemetery, she is now in a position to use her experiences to help other parents who have recently lost a baby. "You just have to tell them that it doesn't get easier, but you do learn to cope with it. It never goes away."

Claire and Marc regularly post photographs and updates to a Facebook page she has dedicated to her firstborn son. They both find it therapeutic, as well as helping keep Jack alive in the memories of friends and family. A shelf in their bedroom is adorned with photographs of him. They leaf proudly through an album, which holds a lock of Jack's hair, cut-outs of memorial notices placed in the local paper, and the hat that he wore whilst in special care, complete with small holes cut for the tubes to run through.

Jack's grave is regularly visited by his family. They change the flowers, tidy up the gravel, and clean the headstone. "It's like when you have a living child and you decorate their room," explains Claire. "That place is special for Jack. It's his place. We owe him the same things that we're doing for Holly and Harvey."

A big regret for Claire is that she never got to see the colour of Jack's eyes. But she, Marc, Holly and Harvey will forever have him as a huge part of their lives. They do not take anything for granted now; a lot of things have been put into perspective. And, once a week, Claire will go to 'Jack's', and tell him about her day.

Do Not Stand at my Grave and Weep

by Mary E. Frye

Do not stand any my grave and weep,
I am not there, I do not sleep.
I am the thousand winds that blow.
I am diamond glints on snow.
I am the sunlight on ripened grain.
I am gentle Autumnal rain.
When you awaken in the morning's hush,
I am the soft uplifting rush
Of quiet birds in circled flight.
I am the soft stars that shine at night.
Do not stand at my grave and cry.
I am not there, I did not die.

Baby Billings

Paula Billings smiles as she remembers her youth. "Everyone in our school, and in our time, could dance," she says. "If we go out now, there's a lot of married couples like us; you never see them propping up the bar, they're always dancing."

Even now, forty years later, Paula confesses to "a bit of rock and roll" with her husband John, who she met at school when he came over from Ireland. John has always been a good dancer, and Paula remembers the time when she and her best friend Jane would attend school socials and keep their fingers crossed that John Billings would ask them to dance. "He'd ask me," she recalls, "and then he'd dance with her." A bit of friendly competition, it seems – but there were no hard feelings when John and Paula married in 1969: Jane was her chief bridesmaid.

Paula was twenty when she married; eighteen months later she started at teacher training college in Newbold Revel, in a building which is now used to train prison officers. She was the first person in her family to ever go to college. "I thought college was something Americans did in books I read," she says. "I didn't know anybody who'd ever been to college or university."

In the second year of her course Paula fell pregnant. "I was feeling sick at college," she recalls. "I stayed overnight with some friends, and then took a pregnancy test the next morning. Of course, all the girls thought it was great!"

Paula, her parents and her two sisters had a family meeting, and decided that they would look after the baby between them so that she could finish her education. Her college friends offered to babysit during lectures.

Surrounded by this close-knit support, Paula describes her pregnancy as "brilliant". She was in fantastic physical condition, cycling to college or running for the bus even when seven months pregnant. Her due date came and went, and when she was a fortnight overdue the decision was made that she would be induced. She was admitted to hospital on a Sunday, and told that she would be induced the next day.

"I was so optimistic. I'd got all this fruit, and food and stuff. The doctor said: 'What's all that?', and I said, 'It's for my husband, to keep him going!'" she laughs. "I'd got lovely nightclothes and perfume, and I said to myself 'I don't care how bad it is, afterwards you have a baby. It's worth it.'"

Unfortunately, Paula's optimism was misplaced. On the Monday, an emergency patient came in and her induction was delayed. The same thing happened on Tuesday. Finally, she was taken into the labour ward on Wednesday, where a doctor struggled to insert a cannula into Paula's forearm. "I looked, and there was blood everywhere. He couldn't get the needle in."

Finally, the cannula was inserted, and Paula was hooked up to a drip which fed a labour-inducing hormone into her bloodstream. A few hours later, a nurse entered the room and asked if Paula was having any contractions. "I said, 'every minute, and they're lasting for a minute'," she remembers. "She looked at me, and said 'oh, don't be ridiculous'."

Despite her reservations, the nurse proceeded to carry out an inspection, which Paula remembers well. "She said, 'Oh, yes, that's a contraction', and she went to leave, and said, 'Oh, that's another one...'"

Paula was in full-blown labour, but had always said that she didn't want any drugs. However, time was passing, and the hospital staff eventually gave her something to help dull the pain. What it was, Paula cannot remember, but what she does recall is its effect. "I lost it. I didn't know where I was, I didn't know what I was doing." She had, during pregnancy, done much research into breathing techniques, which differ depending on which stage of childbirth the mother has reached.

"I said: 'Which stage am I at, how am I supposed to be breathing?' 'That's a load of rubbish', they said, 'they tell you all these stupid things, but you can't get away from it: labour hurts, and that's it'."

The maternity staff tried to give Paula gas and air, but it kept coming away in her hand. "I ended up throwing it at the nurse." Shortly afterwards, she began hallucinating, and could see insects running up the walls. The midwives, unaware of this, asked Paula if she would like John to come back into the room – they'd previously sent him out, as was the norm at the time.

"I said 'No, he can't come back to all this mess'," Paula recalls. "They said 'What mess?', and I said 'It's filthy, all these insects crawling up the walls and everything'. I just lost the plot, I couldn't do anything."

Nine hours after beginning labour at 11am, Paula had barely progressed; fortunately, though, her baby – which had been breech – had now turned. She vaguely remembers a doctor at the foot of her bed becoming increasingly frustrated that Paula, who stands just shy of five feet tall, was giving birth naturally. "I was actually booked in for a home birth," says Paula, "and I think if

I'd had one, I'd have been alright, because they'd have known something was going wrong, and sent me into hospital for a Caesarean section straight away."

Paula asked the doctor why he didn't give her a C-section, or at least use forceps, but she cannot remember his response. A midwife asked her if she was having a contraction. "I said, 'I don't know'. They said, 'This is really important, because we can't feel the baby's heartbeat, and if you're having a contraction it could be muffling it.' I kind of knew then, and I just went cold."

Eventually, at just after midnight, Paula was admitted for a Caesarean section; which, at the time, was carried out under general anaesthetic. She awoke the next morning at around 8am. The curtains were pulled around the bed, and the room was dark and gloomy. She could hear two nurses talking to one another.

"In my mind, when I came round, I kept saying, 'Clare, Clare, Clare', the name I thought we'd call our baby if it was a girl. I was aware that there were nurses in the room, and I thought 'they're not talking to me, the baby must be dead'."

When the nurses had gone, John came through the curtains. He was crying as he held Paula's hand. Their child had been stillborn. She asked what her baby girl was like.

"Why do you keep saying 'she'?" said John. Paula had given birth to a boy, something which at the time pleased her very much. "When I was six, we had a brother, but he died when he was ten days old. My dad really missed having a boy, and my two older sisters both had boys, so I thought I'd never have one. John said it was the most beautiful baby he'd ever seen, perfect looking."

Paula asked if she could see her son, but was told by the midwives that it would be too upsetting. "They don't do it like that nowadays."

Paula had lost a lot of blood during her Caesarean section, and was very anaemic. She came round from the operation on a Thursday, but it was Monday before she felt well enough to suggest to John that they should begin organising a funeral for their baby.

"He said, 'I hope you don't mind, but we had the funeral on Friday'. It had already happened. I thought, 'Oh, that can't be helped'."

Was Paula not angry that the funeral had taken place without her? "No, I wasn't at all," she responds. "I wasn't really with it then. I just think that people did what they thought was best."

Her son had been baptised by a midwife as the operation progressed whilst still in Paula's womb, and so was buried by the priest at her local church. Paula's mother and one of her sisters stood outside the churchyard as John went to the funeral with his father-in-law. Their son was buried in the same grave as an old man, who was of no relation. This did upset Paula at the time, especially when she discovered that her mother was going to ask John if he wanted to bury their baby in the same grave as her brother, but decided against it as she didn't want to upset him. "I would much rather my baby was buried in my brother's grave, as opposed to that of some old man."

Paula was in hospital for a week, the doctors discharging her even though her anaemia was still so severe she was experiencing difficulties with her vision. At one point the number of tubes she was attached to had convinced her family that she may not pull through.

"My dad came to see me, and he would never see anybody in hospitals," she remembers. "Mum made him come to see me. Everything was so hushed the day I woke up; I looked at John, and he was in such a state, and I said 'Am I going to die?' He said, 'No, for goodness' sake, you're not going to die!' But my mum thought I was, because she'd never seen all these drips before."

When looking back at the weeks and months following the death of her son, Paula focuses on the positives. "In some ways, the year afterwards was one of the happiest," she explains. "John and I were really close, he was really supportive, everyone was really kind. People would ask me what I'd had, but friends would explain the situation on my behalf. Then they'd feel really awful and say 'I'm really sorry', but I would say, 'Oh, no, thank you for asking.'"

'Happiest' is perhaps the wrong word, but looking back Paula can see that the whole experience, as heart-breaking as it was – and is – has made her a better person. "We all have challenges in our lives, and sometimes tragedies," she says, "but it's how we react to them and learn from them that makes us better human beings."

Paula has always been vibrant and positive, and she felt she had to display this façade even during tragic and troublesome times. She was cracking jokes during labour; when the midwives commented on the strength of her stomach muscles, she responded "That's because I do gym. Gym as in 'gymnastics', not Jim the man!"

But in private she and John were consumed with grief. One of Paula's friends from college visited her when she was recovering at home, and was pleasantly surprised to see her making jokes and seeming breezy. "When he left I just burst into tears, and said to John 'I can't do this any more, it's too much of a strain.'"

Even nowadays the grief will return, often at the most unexpected times. Once she drove to the school where she worked and started crying in the car when she arrived. More recently she and John were watching TV; the storyline was uncannily similar to her own experiences.

"The atmosphere in the room changed, you could just tell," she says. "I crept along the sofa to John and put my head on his shoulder, and we both started crying. We couldn't speak for a while, until he said to me, 'It's good to remember'."

*

Paula and John were expecting their firstborn baby in 1972. They had prepared for becoming parents; and so, when their baby was taken away from them, they were keen to try again. "You're ready for your whole life to change, you're going to go from being a couple to a family, and even though I was at college we'd managed to work around it – and then there's nothing, and you go back home. The thing is, you don't just lose your son; you lose his wife, you lose his children. Now, I have six grandchildren – but who knows? It could have been eight."

It was a year later when Paula first discovered that she was pregnant once again. She and John moved house, upsizing to a property with three bedrooms, one of which was a nursery, populated with both brand new pieces of furniture as well as hand-me-downs.

Despite her previous loss, Paula remembers being optimistic when she found out she was pregnant with her second child. The doctors had assured her whilst she was recovering from her first pregnancy that should she expect another baby she would be well looked after. Pre-natal care in the 1970s, however, consisted of an initial check-up three months into the pregnancy, followed by a second at seven months. This is what was given to Paula, who complained to one of the members of staff and was allocated an additional appointment.

The doctors were puzzled as to why Paula had returned before her scheduled seven-month appointment, and it was only when she explained her situation that they understood. During the appointment it transpired that Paula's pelvis was not in as good condition as first thought. Instead of the usual funnel-shaped tunnel tapering down from the hips, the gap in Paula's pelvis was the same diameter at the top as it was at the bottom.

"I asked the doctor what this meant, to which he replied 'The baby could get stuck, so we might have to use forceps.' I said, 'You needn't think I'm lying there for thirteen hours again, just so you can use forceps and give me a brain-damaged child.'"

Paula vividly remembers the doctor rolling his eyes and leaving the room to fetch a consultant, who entered, read her notes, and booked her in for a Caesarean. This was carried out when Paula was full term, again under general anaesthetic, and her daughter Shelley was born, alive and well.

Paula would go on to have two more children – two boys – again by Caesarean section. When she had her youngest, John-Paul, in 1977, she requested an epidural as opposed to general anaesthetic. The hospital staff asked her where she'd heard about epidurals; TV, said Paula. "That's just a gimmick for television," said the midwife, and once again she was placed under general anaesthetic.

When she came round from the operation, she was amazed to find that she was given a bed on the ward next to the twin sister of a woman she had met when she gave birth to her firstborn. In another bizarre coincidence, the nurse on duty at the time was the same nurse who admitted her when she was entering the hospital to give birth to her first child. Paula was the last person the nurse saw before moving onto the labour ward, and was now the first person she attended to upon her return.

Because Paula had all of her children by Caesarean section, and was first into theatre on each occasion, they all celebrate their birthday at 10 in the morning. On 21st September – the anniversary of the birth of her first child – she tells her children that it would have been their older brother's birthday, and they talk about him. Shelley thinks about how things may have been different if she was not the eldest; perhaps he would have brought home friends that she would have had a crush on, maybe even married.

Paula thinks back to her teenage years and comments on how selfish she feels she was. "You take things for granted. You're a kid, everything goes your way, you get married, you're sailing along, then you have a baby. But losing a child makes you wake up, it makes you realise that life doesn't just work like that. And I think I became a less selfish person.

"In some ways I think it changed me for the better. I gained things. I haven't spent the last thirty-nine years being upset and miserable at all, and I've had three great kids."

It took five years after her son's death for Paula to ask John whether they had a birth or death certificate, and another few years for her to request a copy from the local authority. It was a combined birth and death certificate, and listed the cause of death as asphyxia; but Paula found comfort in the fact that she finally had a piece of paper which told her that her son was born, was real, and not just a memory.

Paula has never seen the boy she lost almost forty years ago. Most of the past few years have been spent trying to find the plot in which her son is buried, but memories of the exact location have faded and records are sparse. She has a few people to call, but something quiet, something unknown keeps holding her back. Still, she is resolute to find the resting place of her son before what would have been his fortieth birthday; and, when she does, she plans on placing an angel on his grave as a permanent memorial to her son, whose death changed her and her husband forever, and for the better.

'Sticky Bean's Siblings

When Emily Davidson graduated from university and took a job as a barmaid at the Font & Firkin in Brighton, she didn't end up just pulling pints. She also found the love of her life in Dan; and, fifteen years later, they are still going strong.

There is a little bit of debate around who made the first move, though. It was a work night out, and there were a number of factors involved: gin and tonic, for one, as well as Emily's housemates hitting on him. In the end, Emily is adamant that they both made the first move. Dan has a slightly different view on it: "Who made the first move? Her friends!"

Emily is a self-confessed "unromantic", and so the best date she and Dan went on does not spring to mind easily – although she does wistfully talk about how much she enjoys his company when "it's just the two of us". He quotes a birthday picnic they had one year at South Downs; but the one date which really sticks in Emily's mind is the first time they went out together after their son, Noah, was born. She thought they were going to Pizza Express, but in fact Dan had booked them a table at Delia Smith's restaurant, at Norwich City FC.

Nights out for the two of them are few and far between now they are parents; but, when they first became an item, they had eleven years without having to worry about dirty nappies, or routines, or school uniforms. But then the small blue lines on a pregnancy test confirmed that Emily was six weeks pregnant. She can't remember exactly how she told Dan the news: she either left the test on the worktop for Dan to find, or "popped it into conversation when he got home from work."

Either way, it was good news: Emily and Dan had been trying for a baby for six months. She had always wanted two children, but Dan had envisaged four. Neither were particularly intent on achieving their respective numbers, so in the end they settled on three. With baby number one, they would be a third of the way there.

However, their happiness was sadly short-lived. The day after taking the test Emily began to suffer cramps. "I was on holiday from work and had just got a kitten," she says. "I went to my friends for coffee, and while I was there started to get a period-like pain. I went to the loo, and there was some blood.

"I went home, and cried. I spent the afternoon on the sofa, hoping that things weren't ending, but they were. I went to the doctor the next day, and he did a pregnancy test which confirmed I wasn't pregnant any more. I was still bleeding, and did for a few days."

Like so many couples who long to be parents yet have had the opportunity taken away, Emily and Dan were intent on becoming pregnant again as quickly as possible. "After trying for six months, I knew my cycle inside out. You can't help but count the days."

Emily fell pregnant again soon after she suffered a miscarriage – "too quickly" she says, in hindsight. Finding out was still a happy occurrence for her and Dan, but it was somewhat diluted. "I felt quite negative about it," she remembers, "but think that was just because of what had happened before, and I was trying not to get excited."

Emily found out in September that she was pregnant. A few weeks later, at eleven weeks, she was relaxing on the first Saturday of the October half-term, when she noticed that she had a little bleeding. Concerned, she rang the midwife, who told her to rest as much as possible. "The bleeding was on-off on the Saturday and Sunday," she recalls. "I went to work on the Monday and spent the day in a bit of a trance. I hadn't told anyone I was pregnant."

In the early hours of Tuesday morning, the bleeding became heavier and the cramps which characterised Emily's first pregnancy returned. "I knew it was over."

The midwife arranged for an early scan on the Wednesday morning, which showed a clear picture of a baby but no heartbeat. Taken into a side room, Emily and Dan were told that they had suffered a missed miscarriage, and given their options as to what they could do next.

"There was a lot of information about the fact that it wasn't over," remembers Emily. "I had to decide whether to have a medical procedure to remove the pregnancy, use drugs to bring on bleeding or wait for it to happen naturally. I couldn't take it in and asked to be left with the information and call them later."

After a lot of thought, Emily decided that she should have the procedure, under general anaesthetic. She was booked in to have the operation on the Friday following her scan, and took the following week off work. Emily remembers the time well: "It was all just awful."

That's not to say she didn't enjoy seeing her gallows humour make a junior doctor squirm uncomfortably. Emily, Dan and a nurse were joking about an article she was reading which demonstrated how poor men are at identifying areas on a diagram of a woman's reproductive organs. As they joked about this the young doctor was carrying out an internal examination. "I guess it must have seemed odd to the doctor that on such an awful day we were laughing," chuckles Emily, "but you do, don't you?"

The 30th January – three months later – brought news of Emily's third pregnancy in seven months. She had been speculating as to whether or not she was pregnant for a few days, but Dan was reluctant to do a test. Emily took one, but didn't tell Dan for three days – it was positive.

"I was negative and nervous and obsessed the whole time, constantly thinking I could feel bleeding." she says; and, tragically, she suffered a miscarriage three days later. "Everything felt depressingly familiar."

Emily continued to have positive pregnancy tests for the rest of the week, a searing reminder of what had been lost. At the time, Emily kept a journal of her emotions. Her entries at the time reveal how tentative she was before her third miscarriage, and the emotions which followed.

Thursday 31st January 2008
It has been 36 hours and I have yet to have a moment when my positive pregnancy test hasn't been somewhere towards the back or often the front of my mind. Mckdad is still blissfully unaware, lucky for him, I wish I was blissfully unaware. I have to keep chanting 'one day at a time' although 'one hour at a time' would be more appropriate. There is nothing I can do whatever happens. I know there is no guarantee of a baby at the end of it, but I can't help thinking there might be.

Tuesday 5ᵗʰ February 2008
My world has crashed around me for the third time in 7
months and I have learned that holding your excitement in
makes the devastation no easier.

Emily and Dan had suffered three miscarriages and they had taken their toll, both physically and mentally. "I really started to think that I wouldn't be able to have children, and felt like a total failure as a woman," she explains. "I was annoyed I'd left it so late to try, as I'd been focused on my career. I was in despair."

By April, Emily's doctor had signed her off work due to bereavement, and referred her to their local Pregnancy Crisis Centre. He explained that she had not managed to cope fully with each setback, was not going through the grieving process, and as such had dipped further each time she suffered a miscarriage.

Dan tried to stay philosophical throughout the turbulent months, and appeared to be taking it all quite well: "Which irritated me", says Emily. However, Dan may not have been coping as well as it seemed he was. Like many mourning fathers, his grief was a more private occurrence.

"He went into himself," recalls Emily, "not that I noticed. He spent too much time on the computer or watching films, and stayed up late. We drifted apart a little; but once I got really low and was signed off work, he was brilliant."

The majority of hospital staff were equally as brilliant, Emily describing them as "sensitive and supportive". However, the doctor they saw after suffering the third miscarriage was "totally dismissive". Emily and Dan sought a reason as to why they were experiencing so many setbacks, but left empty-handed. "He said it was either a problem with antibodies or genetics, in which case there would be nothing they could do," recalls Emily, frustrated. "My GP had already ruled out an antibody issue, but I had to have blood taken again. This doctor basically told us to keep trying and come back in six months. He wasn't prepared to look into genetic issues at all."

Emily felt a great sense of injustice at her losses, when compared to other mothers who seemed to have uneventful and happy pregnancies. "It seemed I was surrounded by pregnant women and pushchairs," she remembers. "There are so many baby name books on the shelves but nothing on miscarriage. Surely they all have John, Mary and Jake in them. Why do we need so many?!"

Whilst many may have given up after experiencing the tragedy of three miscarriages, Emily and Dan were resolute that they wanted to be parents – and this became the source of their strength. By Emily's own admission, she has managed to "make stuff happen" throughout her life – exams, jobs, relationships – but when it came to becoming a mother she had failed, which frustrated and angered her. Not only this, but Emily also felt that she was somehow letting Dan down. "I knew he desperately wanted to be a dad, and I felt as though I was failing him somehow."

Many friends were supportive – especially Emily's best friend, who she says was "brilliant" – but some people said the wrong thing, often inadvertently. "They would say nothing, or things like 'Well, at least you can get pregnant', as if the goal was getting pregnant, not having a healthy child."

Emily's father, too, gave some misplaced advice. When she and Dan found out that one of Dan's friends was pregnant, it upset Dan; and Emily mentioned this to her father. "He told me:

'You can't get annoyed at people getting on with their lives'."

Whilst Emily's friendship with her best friend grew stronger, some friendships fell by the wayside. One friend in particular always seemed to say the wrong thing, and was the assistant to Emily's "less than supportive" boss, who refused to agree to reducing Emily's hours after she lost her second baby, stating that "What had happened to me happened to lots of people, and they didn't need time off."

Emily received counselling, which turned out to be the most helpful thing that she could have done. Her counsellor, Tash, had some words of advice, which certainly hit home.

"She told me that I should imagine my tears filling a glass." recalls Emily. "Eventually they would stop, but until the glass was full they needed to come out. She explained that, at some point, I would be able to think of the losses without feeling the pain."

Tash also encouraged Emily to write about her emotions, in journal and letter form: she states that it "saved me". As part of her counselling, she wrote a letter to each of her unborn children. "I treasure these, as they felt like the proper goodbye that I never gave them when I lost them."

*

A few months later, Dan was a few days into travelling around Europe with his sister when he received a phone call from Emily. At the time, he was in Croatia, and had just returned from a bike ride during which someone had opened their car door and knocked him off his bike. He was told that they were expecting a child.

Emily had decided to take the news of her fourth pregnancy

differently to those previously experienced, and even gave her unborn baby a nickname. "I had realised there was no point in being negative, as it made no difference to the outcome and expecting the worst did not protect you when the worst happened. I decided that I had to stay positive, and started referring to him as 'Sticky Bean' as soon as I found out."

With Dan being away, Emily was on her own for a few weeks; but refers to it as a "good thing" – not because Dan was absent, but because she could rely on her own inner strength to galvanise her positive outlook and help her through the first few weeks of pregnancy. She checked for bleeding often, of course, and refrained from buying anything for many months; but endeavoured to have a strong and optimistic attitude throughout. Even Emily's friends and family noticed a difference in her behaviour.

"They had learned to be pleased and yet not too excited when they heard the news," she explains, "but they did take it a little differently this time, because they realised that I felt differently; that even if the worst happened I was stronger and would be able to handle it."

Because of her previous history, Emily was given early scans by a midwife who was "brilliant"; and the sonographers themselves were "really sensitive and encouraging about what they saw." Emily's excitement grew as time passed, but she refused to get carried away. "I took each day as it came. Occasionally I would have a day where I was nervous, but generally I forced myself to stay positive."

Deciding that she wanted to be a stay-at-home-mum, Emily took early maternity leave, resolute that she would not return once her time off work was complete. It gave her time to relax –

although she didn't particularly enjoy the pregnancy. "I felt sick until about fourteen weeks, and then had a horrible sickness bug for a week at nineteen weeks, and was grumpy for most of it."

Emily awoke at 5am on her due date to her waters breaking, and – upon advice from the hospital – was told to go in that evening if no significant progress had been made. The afternoon brought mild contractions, but "nothing to get excited about", and so she and Dan made their way to the hospital. After a few hours of monitoring they were sent home to wait some more: tired, but pleased that their 'Sticky Bean' had a strong heartbeat.

The next day came, and – although Emily's contractions were a bit more painful – no progress had been made; and so they returned to hospital. An examination was carried out, which revealed that Emily was only three centimetres dilated; and so, once again, they returned home to wait. Emily sums up that day – Easter Sunday – in a few words: "Old episodes of *Friends*, contractions, a birthing ball, dancing to the baby's iPod playlist in an attempt to get things moving, a TENS machine, and *lots* of maternity pads."

Once home, Emily went to bed as Dan remained downstairs. At 1am, just as Dan was ready to get into bed, she informed him that the contractions were much worse, and they had to return to hospital. "He wasn't best pleased," she recalls with a smile. "I seem to remember him actually asking if I was sure or just joking!"

This time Emily knew that she would not be sent home again. The contractions were strong enough to stop her from walking when they came, although they were irregular. During her stay, she was looked after by three midwives, whom she refers to as "lovely". Each one took note of her birth plan and stuck to it, even refusing Emily gas and air when the contractions became more intense. Eventually, they broke her waters; and, after the midwife "changed her clothes and the bedsheets, and mopped the floor – we'll say no more about that… " it was time to start pushing.

Their baby was taking his time in making an entrance, and Emily quickly became "demoralised, tired and emotional". But spare a thought for Dan: it was his task to press the boost button on Emily's TENS machine every time she had a contraction, which he did for four hours straight – something which, he points out was "very difficult, what with all the concentrating and staying awake."

Emily gave herself a pep talk as she entered the final stages of childbirth. "I put my head in my hands and went very quiet," she says. "I turned inwards and told myself I had to find some strength from somewhere. I was reminding myself that I'd wanted this for so long and it was nearly over; that I had to do it and that I could do it, even through I was finding the pushing the most difficult and painful part of labour."

Eventually, after encouragement from a midwife, a "fresh faced jolly doctor" and a "slightly scary midwife sister", Noah was born, weighing 6lb 12oz. Emily vividly remembers the relief and ecstasy she felt: "It had taken fifty-two hours, two sets of TENS pads, four midwives, a doctor, a brilliant partner and zero drugs, but we were finally done.

"I felt a rush of so many different emotions: joy, shock and relief all mixed together with the practicalities that are going on all around. I couldn't stop gazing at this tiny creature who celebrated his entry into the world with a feed and a lovely sleep."

Emily and Dan finally had a boy to hold in their arms; but he wouldn't be the first. When Noah was seventeen months old, she fell pregnant. "This is when I realised that I *really* don't like being pregnant!" remembers Emily. "I was so tired and sick until about sixteen weeks, and grumpy at the end. In fact, I didn't really feel myself throughout."

However, her bad experiences of pregnancy were largely forgotten when Elijah was born, after a slightly traumatic childbirth which saw him being born with meconium in his water and the cord wrapped around his neck and body. However, after a bit of time beneath a heater, and with a lot of "skin time", his temperature reached a normal level, and he was fine. Twelve hours later, Emily and Dan returned home with their newborn boy.

Emily's losses have dramatically changed her attitude on life. "Before my miscarriages I was a career girl, climbing the ladder and earning good money doing it. It was long hours, and stressful. I didn't really enjoy it, but was planning on returning after maternity leave.

"After my losses, I came to the conclusion that life is too short, having children is not a given and they are small for such a short time – so I became a full-time mother. I feel so lucky to have had two healthy boys, and before I had miscarriages I think I just took it for granted that I would be a mum. I have realised that you can't control everything, and that will alone does not make things happen. As a result I am more relaxed than I think I have ever been. I know what a massive journey each of my boys has had to make just to get here."

Emily is thankful that she has a good GP, who recognises that the effects of miscarriage extend beyond what you can see or touch. "Doctors, nurses and midwives need to pay more attention to the emotional side of miscarriage, even if it is just a referral to an appropriate support group or counselling."

As well as improving post-loss care for parents, Emily also feels that the medical language and terminology should be reviewed. "Even if medically it is a foetus, to a parent it is already a baby," she clarifies. "For example, the operation I had is called 'an evacuation of retained products of conception'."

No new parent wants to be told that something could go wrong; but Emily believes that people should certainly be made more aware of miscarriage, if only to help lift the taboo which currently surrounds all forms of infant death, whether it be miscarriage, stillbirth or neonatal death. "As with most things that are taboo, people just don't know what to say for the best, and so everyone just remains quiet. Sadness is brushed under the carpet."

There are still days when the grief of losing three babies returns; perhaps if a certain song is playing, or if a family friend suffers a similar tragedy. But writing has proven to be the perfect remedy for Emily, and she now blogs regularly (mummylimited.blogspot.com). "I have moments when I think about my losses," she says, "but if I do I usually write, shed a few tears and then hug one or both of my children a little tighter and make a cup of tea."

Emily encourages other parents in a similar situation to not ignore their losses, and to give themselves the time they need. "Respect your own feelings. Whether you move on quickly or need to grieve, either is perfectly normal and acceptable."

Both Emily and Dan have trod an arduous journey over the past few years. On the wall in Eli's nursery hang three pairs of bootees: a gentle yet perfect symbol to demonstrate that, even though they have two happy and healthy children, they will never forget the babies they lost.

Extracts From My Journal
by Emily Davidson

A Letter to my Second Baby
It has been eight months since I lost you. Your birth date has been and gone and still I can't let you go. I miss you although I never saw you. For a long time I didn't want to let you go and in a way I still don't but for the most part I want to go forward and you, or rather I, am stopping that. Tash [my counsellor] says imagine a cup of tears and once it is full there are no more. Somehow I have to say goodbye to you because, you see, I can't try again until I have.

Monday 16th March, 2010 (when pregnant with Noah)
I am having my coffee in the garden for the 1st time this year. Another reminder that Spring is here and baby will be here soon too. I cannot really believe we are here. A year ago I was in a dreadful state and didn't believe things would change. Now, at last, baby will be here soon and I'll have all I wanted.

Sunday 7th June (a few months after Noah's birth)
The weeks have gone so fast. I think the fastest ever.

He is here and I still cannot really believe it. Everything that happened before seems so long ago. Even pregnancy and giving birth, which is why I should be writing. I feel as though I want to hold onto every moment and keep it for a bit longer.

Of course it has not all been easy and wonderful. I am no different; still incredibly hard on myself, still listening to those unwanted voices making me doubt myself.

However, I am different in some ways. I have unconditional, unselfish love for him and want to do my absolute best for him.

Finley

If you were to ask Mel Scott which date with her husband, Baz, was her favourite, there would be no contest. They had gone ten-pin bowling, and he was becoming increasingly frustrated that she was winning. "He wanted to get a strike, but misthrew," she recalls, with a grin. "The ball went into the gutter, so he ran after it to pretend to kick it. His legs went up over his head, and he fell over!"

An example, then, of just one of the many enjoyable times that Mel and Baz have shared in their ten years together. However, they may never have met at all, were it not for Mel's friends dragging her out to a nightclub in Plymouth. Having just split up with her boyfriend of seven years, she was understandably not in the dancing mood, but was eventually persuaded. It was there that she saw Baz.

"A very drunk me sat next to him and talked at him for several hours," she recollects. "The next day he came home with me and never left!" But who made the first move? "Erm… I don't remember. But I was drunk, so probably me!"

Being able to communicate with people in any state of sobriety has always been Mel's strong point; and is a virtue which she uses often in her career as an occupational therapist, teacher, life coach and author. "As part of my degree in occupational therapy and during my job working in mental health services, I enjoyed running workshops and training days, so trained to be a post-sixteen teacher. The life coaching happened very naturally."

Little did Mel know that one day the skills that she had acquired in her training would help her learn to cope with her own grief, and also be a source of support for others. It was a few days before Mother's Day when she discovered she was pregnant with their first child.

"My friend called me to say she was pregnant, and I realised I hadn't had a period for a while," she says. "I bought a pack of tests and then ran into our bedroom and jumped on the bed screaming at Baz 'I'm pregnant!'"

They'd been trying for six months with no luck, and it was only after five more positive tests – including a digital one – that Baz finally believed the good news. "He got really excited!"

Mel was also understandably ecstatic at being six weeks pregnant; so much so that she wasted no time in telling a lot of her family and friends the good news. "I remember a work friend asking how far gone I was, and I told her. She said I shouldn't be telling people yet, but I thought nothing could happen."

However, just a few days after finding out she was pregnant, Mel started spotting. The doctors in the local hospital Accident & Emergency department examined her and stated that she was not miscarrying, and that – instead of being six weeks pregnant – Mel was eight weeks along. However, to be sure, they organised an appointment with the Early Pregnancy Unit (EPU), who concluded that there was a baby present, but that it was not the correct size for eight weeks.

At this point, the bleeding had stopped, but the EPU staff carried out a blood test to check Mel's Human Chorionic Gonadotrophin (HCG) levels, which is detected at high levels during the early weeks of pregnancy. Any HCG reading over twenty-five indicates pregnancy: Mel's levels read seventy. A second blood test was taken a couple of days later, and the HCG reading should have doubled; but they remained at seventy.

The staff suspected a miscarriage, but carried out a third blood test to check Mel's progesterone levels. "I went back with my mum and friend to the hospital, and they said that the progesterone level was not high enough to support a pregnancy." It was confirmed that Mel had, unfortunately, suffered a miscarriage.

There were three options: have a dilation and curettage operation, commonly referred to as a D&C; take a tablet to speed along the natural process; or simply wait for nature to take its course. Mel chose the third option, and a few days later the bleeding and cramping indicated the end of the distressing process. Mel went to work as she waited for the cramping to begin: "I didn't know what else to do."

After she and Baz had miscarried, Mel rang work and phoned in sick, staying off for three weeks. The hospital staff, although nice during Mel's appointments, did little to acknowledge their loss and what it meant to her and Baz. She was given a leaflet, but it was not enough. Her friends were very supportive, speaking to her about what happened; some, however, spoke very little of the miscarriage, and expected Mel to 'get on with it'.

Mel's best friend, Annette, took her shopping on the day she went for her final blood test results, and suggested that she buy a ring with that month's birthstone in it. "So I bought a little ring, with three blue topaz stones in it. Later on I looked at it and the shape of the stones almost looked like an angel's wings and body."

Mel also bought a small pair of bootees, and placed them with her positive pregnancy tests. She ordered some keepsakes from an online company: a teddy, a pin badge, and a silver heart charm, which Baz wears. All of these items formed a physical reminder of their first baby, cherished to this day.

Seven months after their loss, Mel's friend – whose phone call had prompted her to take a pregnancy test – gave birth. It was the day which Mel had calculated would have been her due date. "I went to meet her and her new baby in hospital," remembers Mel, "and I just held him and cried and cried."

It was not just that her friend's baby reminded Mel of her own lost child. She and Baz had been trying to get pregnant again for a while, and were finding it difficult. Seeing her friend's child prompted Mel to tell her husband that it was just too hard, too difficult to conceive, and that they should stop. "Having a period every month was just like having another miscarriage."

*

It was just after they'd decided to stop trying, however, when Mel discovered that she was pregnant. This time, there was no jumping on the bed.

"I was scared," says Mel. "We didn't tell anyone until after twelve weeks. I had a scan at eight weeks, in which I basically lied and said I had been bleeding, because I had to know it was okay, and it was so long to wait until twelve weeks."

The eight-week scan showed a baby which, in Mel's words, "looked like a little sea horse." The twelve-week scan, however, showed a little baby with its hand behind its head; a sight which broke the guards which Mel and Baz had built to protect them from further heartache and resulted in them both being "so excited."

The pregnancy, Mel says, was wonderful. "My friend had given me a book called *The Gentle Birth Method*, which looks at different ways to prepare for a natural birth like homeopathy, nutrition, exercise and hypnotherapy. I listened to a pregnancy relaxation CD every day, had homeopathy, Reiki and reflexology every week, swam four times a week, and ate well. I had no problems at all."

Mel and Baz decided not to find out the sex of their baby in the twenty-week scan, instead choosing a name each: Baz chose a boy's name, Mel a girl's. "He came up with a load of very dodgy names," smiles Mel, "and Finley was the only one we both liked. Alfie came a close second, but my mum said she knew a very naughty Alfie!"

Mel was over forty-one weeks pregnant when her waters broke. She turned on her relaxation CD and rang the hospital, who told her to come in. By the time she and Baz arrived at the hospital there was meconium in her waters; but she was not dilated at all, and was having no contractions.

"They checked my baby's heart on the trace monitor: it was fine. Because the labour ward was full, and I was not in established labour, they admitted me to the antenatal ward and sent Baz home."

At about 3am, the meconium was thicker and Mel was suffering mild contractions. Still not dilated, she asked the hospital staff to turn the heart monitor back on. An hour later, and having noticed that her baby's heart rate was dropping, she called the midwife. It was nearly two hours later, at 5.45am, when an ultrasound was carried out and a slow heart beat was found. An emergency Caesarean was ordered; and it was during this operation that Finley died.

Mel had a general anaesthetic, and came round to the news that they had a boy but that he had been stillborn. Baz, called by the hospital staff and summoned to hospital, arrived after the operation. He helped the midwife bathe and dress Finley, which they videoed as Mel was still asleep at the time. Their parents visited, and had photographs taken with him.

Mel and Baz spent three days in hospital with Finley, and he stayed in the room with them the whole time. They had him blessed, gave him a teddy bear and dressed him in different clothes. "The last night one of the midwives helped me to decide how to say goodbye, so I got to bathe him, dress him, read him a story and tuck him in his cot."

The first two weeks after Finley's death were spent organising his funeral. "I barely slept or ate," says Mel, "I wanted it to be perfect." The night before the funeral, Mel and Baz brought Finley home. The funeral went well: Mel says that it "amazed her", and over a hundred family members and friends attended. "Most people did not know what to say or do, but the fact that they bothered to come helped. It was hugely supportive."

The funeral, despite being a source of great comfort, was followed by months which Mel found particularly difficult. Although she had some good days – "days where I managed to eat, go out and not cry" – most of her time was taken up with a crushing sadness.

"I couldn't breathe, I ached all over, my stomach felt one minute like there was a baby in it, and the next that it was empty. It felt very lonely."

Despite her feelings of loneliness, Mel found that she and Baz grew much closer in the months following Finley's death. When Mel suffered from infections as a result of "not looking after myself", Baz would give her injections and medications. "He used to remind me what I was going to do, as I would forget."

But Baz did not feel like talking about Finley; not for the first few months, at least. Mel, on the other hand, wanted to talk about him a lot. But they spent their time together, and went on holiday after four months, having what Mel remembers affectionately as a "beautiful time".

They found that their priorities had changed, that their outlook on life had shifted since their loss. "Things that used to worry us became insignificant. I have much less patience with moaning people who don't know what they have got. I can't keep my mouth shut when people moan about their children, and sometimes will say 'I would do anything to shout at my Finley because he has been naughty; you don't know how lucky you are.'

"I appreciate how precious life is now. I have faith in the world again, the kindness of strangers, the care of a family. I purposefully look for the beauty and the positives now. I have had to learn to see them, but now the sky, rainbows, stars, butterflies… all sorts, has a new meaning."

Friends were a great source of help, some calling frequently to check that she and Baz were okay. Some would visit them, and visit Finley's grave. But Mel soon realised that life moves on for everyone else, despite the fact that it was standing still for her. "Life goes back to normal for them, but there was no normal for me."

As well as receiving support from friends, family, and – of course – Baz ("a huge support just by being there, my rock"), Mel found solace via the Internet. "Facebook was a massive support," she explains, "because in the middle of the night there was always someone to talk to me – even in another country. I have spoken to total strangers on the Internet, who are now close friends."

88

Mel's local baby loss group was far from helpful, unfortunately. Two months after Finley's death she went to her first meeting, and describes it as "horrendous." Several of the other mums were pregnant, and a couple complained about how big their bumps were. "It was all I could do not to scream and punch them."

But she persevered, and still attends the meetings today. Now, she and the three other mums have all gone on to have another child, and so most of their conversation is taken up with talking about them. But at the time, Mel recalls, the lack of thought from other group members hurt so much.

Was Mel ever put under any pressure to 'get over it' following Finley's death? "I *hate* those words." she says, angrily. "I've lost count of how many times people have said I had to let go, move on, move forward, get better. I will do none of those things, except maybe get better. I hated it when people said I was strong. I did not feel strong, I was just surviving as best I could.

"Finley was and is a part of our life. 'Get over it' implies that you forget. I will never forget, and I will make sure that Finley is never forgotten. 'Moving on' implies leaving Finley behind, and that won't happen either. Finley is a part of my life and my family, in a different way to what it would have been had he been alive; but he is still a big part of our life."

Support from hospital staff in the weeks following Finley's death was excellent. "The bereavement midwife was great in the hospital, and visited us after six weeks. We saw the consultant when the reports came back from the post mortem." She was offered counselling, but did not find it proactive enough. Instead of being told how tragic her circumstances were, she wanted someone to help her find hope.

A year after Finley's birth, Mel and Baz placed a '1' made of flowers on the ground and released balloons into the sky whilst standing at his graveside. For his second birthday, they have asked friends to paint a pebble each for him.

*

At the start of 2010, four months after losing Finley, Mel fell pregnant again. It was a planned pregnancy; they had decided as soon as Mel left hospital that they wanted to try again. The news that she was pregnant was met with mixed emotions: "terrified, guilty, happy, nervous, feeling like it was wrong."

Aside from the fear of having to endure the death of another child, Mel worried about bonding with her baby. She worried about whether others would think that she was replacing Finley; indeed, she wondered whether she would forget him altogether. Other people were relieved upon hearing the news that Mel and Baz were expecting their third child: "They thought it would make everything better. Only a few people seemed to understand that we both wanted to be pregnant and not want to be pregnant at the same time because we only wanted Finley."

Hospital staff – knowing of Mel's previous losses – were very supportive. The helpfulness of the midwives and consultants they had with Finley encouraged Mel to insist on having them again. "We chose to have the same midwife, who was wonderful. She would always speak about Finley and cared for me if I cried. She always went with what I wanted; I could go to the hospital every day if I needed to, just to hear the heartbeat. The bereavement midwife changed her shift so that she could be there for the birth. The consultant was the one who gave us our post mortem results;

we chose him because he looked at photos of Finley."

The pregnancy itself, however, was not enjoyable, and Mel found herself in a constant state of anxiety. At one point, near the end of her pregnancy, a midwife mentioned that the baby was not moving much. "That was it," remembers Mel, "I could not control my anxiety. I was a mess. I admitted myself to hospital and spent most of every day on monitors. I asked for a Caesarean, which they did at thirty-seven weeks."

Mel was more knowledgeable this time that things could go wrong. She and the other mothers she had befriended in the weeks following Finley's death were watching every movement, every twinge, for signs that something might be wrong. Mel requested tests that she hadn't even heard of in previous pregnancies, and counted kicks on a daily basis.

In the operating theatre, in preparation for her Caesarean section, Baz turned on an Anastacia CD: "The best of a bad choice," smiles Mel. She had the epidural whilst he held her hand, and remembers a weird feeling and noise when her waters broke. Moments later, their daughter was born.

"I asked the consultant to make sure I was the first to hold Toni-Joi, as this upset me most with Finley, that he was born to strangers and everyone else held him before me. She screamed straight away, which made me cry."

After a few hours, Toni-Joi started to have breathing problems, and was sent to the special care unit. Mel remembers it well.

"Baz went with her, and as soon as they would let me stand up I went to see her. I froze. To see her with all these tubes was awful; a nurse had to make me touch her. Thankfully, she was okay after two days."

Toni-Joi will always know about her older brother. "When we go to see Finley's grave we go to the park as well, so it's fun for her. She has his things in her room."

Mel admits that during her first and second pregnancies she knew very little about the risk of miscarriage and stillbirth, and feels that parents who suffer these tragic events should be given an item to mark their loss, and information on how to remember their baby. Films should feature stillbirth more, she says, and new mums should know the main causes behind this terrible occurrence.

Mel believes that the number of scans and appointments should also increase. "If providing these prevents stillbirth then this should be done for every pregnancy, not just ones after a loss. And all stillborn babies should be bathed, dressed, and placed in a cosy bed or a cold cot, to give their parents time."

Mel kept a diary of her feelings and experiences after Finley's death, and describes this as "a life saver. It meant I could get the thoughts out of my head. It meant I could sleep. It helped me to work out what was happening, and helped me to see what I was learning. Each day ended with a note to Finley, and this helped me keep close to him."

Not only has Mel used her experiences to support her own healing process, but she has set up Finley's Footprints (finleysfootprints.com), an information resource and support service for parents, professionals and charitable organisations involved with the care of bereaved parents and families, and those with terminally ill children. In running Finley's Footprints, Mel uses the skills she learnt during her qualifications and experience as an Occupational Therapist to help and assist others, in organising coaching groups and conferences to bring people together to develop a shared knowledge and understanding.

As well as Finley's Footprints, Mel runs Towards Tomorrow Together (towards-tomorrow.com), a charity which raises money to provide bereaved parents with complementary therapies, and fund coaching and spaces on beneficial workshops.

Mel has some simple words of advice for other parents who find themselves grieving a lost child: "Acknowledge the baby, accept and allow them to be a part of your past, present and future, part of your family.

"Look for the blessings that your baby gives you; the meaning, the random coincidences. The butterfly that comes into your house, the ladybird crawling on you out of season, the rainbow over your baby's resting place. Know that the sadness and despair eases."

As well as ensuring that Finley lives on in the minds of friends and family, Mel has her own special memories of her son, private treasured thoughts which will stay with her forever. "For me, the most precious memory would be lying on a massage couch, having Reiki and feeling him move in my tummy in a way that he would only do when I had relaxation. I loved those times, and feel blessed to have had them. I used to talk to him in my mind during those times. He knows I loved him at that moment."

An Excerpt from After Finley

by Mel Scott

Written the night before Finley's funeral, when he was at home.

To my darling Finley,

Thank you for coming to be with us. You have already made such a big impact on our lives with your short one. I don't think there has ever been another little person who is loved so much.

Your daddy and me love you so very much – the book your Nana gave you says it all. We love you as big as the sky. I know that when you ride your rainbow you will be joining your sister. You make sure you go and play with the horses at the Seven Sisters. We will go there; it's so high we will know you are there with us. We will think of you when we see a rainbow – the beauty in the balance of sunshine and rain – or when we see a candlelight flicker, the rays of sunshine through the clouds, or a butterfly. They say if a butterfly flaps its wings in Australia, a wind blows here – that's just like you. You never got a chance to flap your wings, but you sure made a change in the world.

The world shines for me now; it is full of flickering candles for you, and so much love. I want to thank you for coming to me. I loved being pregnant with you. I know you and all you would have been – all you will still be wherever you are.

94

You are wisdom, peace happiness, joy and love. You are cheeky, mischievous and loveable. You are destined for wonderful things, amazing achievements, and a long, long future teaching others to love without conditions – without regrets. Just as you have taught me and your daddy.

We love you. Without condition; without regret.

Lydia

"Maybe we shouldn't go into too much detail!" Stuart laughs, after being asked how he and his wife, Dawn, first met.

No further questions, then; but the early days of their relationship were not short of romantic – albeit casual – moments. Soon after they began seeing each other, Dawn had to go to America for six months.

"We said 'what will be, will be'," remembers Dawn. "I told Stuart: 'If you're there when I come back, you're there', and we left it at that."

When Dawn returned to London, she was greeted by her parents – yet she couldn't find Stuart's face in the crowd. But then he appeared from behind a pillar, dressed up to the nines in his best suit. A scene from a romantic film, perhaps, complete with swirling background music as the two run towards one another in slow motion?

"Yes," replies Stuart, "except as I go running down the airport, coming towards me would be a twenty-six-tonne truck, because she'd put on that much weight!"

A tongue-in-cheek comment sure to incite wrath; but surprisingly, Dawn agrees. "I'd put on loads of weight, and had a massive backpack on!"

Dawn moved in with Stuart the next day; and, six years later, they got engaged. Was it a romantic proposal? Dawn looks miffed.

"We went out for dinner one night, and he said 'I suppose we'd better get married then. You might as well go and pick your ring.'"

"I'd had a couple of shandies," explains Stuart, "and I thought 'I suppose I'd better ask her'!"

Dawn wanted kids right away, but Stuart was more passive. "I just thought 'if it happens, it happens'. Women are just a completely different make-up, aren't they? But now I do get a bit jealous when I see people who I went to school with who have had kids that are grown-up and have left home, because as you get older you get a bit more selfish in your ways, and you like your free time." With that, he leaves the room to see to a two year-old Emelia, who is whinging at her bedroom door.

Emelia and her twin brother Jenson are the result of years of ups and downs, and several attempts at IVF. Four years after trying naturally with no success, Dawn and Stuart saw a doctor and were referred for treatment, placed on a three-year waiting list.

But a life-threatening accident put paid to any immediate plans of parenthood. Dawn was driving through roadworks on the M42 when she had a head-on collision with a car: both vehicles were driving at 60mph. The car driver escaped with minor injuries; but Dawn's body took the full impact of the force.

"I was mangled," recalls Dawn. "The doctors told Stuart that they were probably going to have to amputate my right arm and left leg. My other arm and leg were both broken, my spleen had to be removed, my pelvis was broken in five places. Both of my lungs were punctured, and I arrested twice in theatre. I shouldn't be here, that's what they tell me."

Dawn was treated in the trauma centre at the Queen Elizabeth Hospital in Birmingham, for which she is now an ambassador. Fortunately, surgeons managed to save Dawn's arm and leg ("Some of the techniques that doctors learned from treating injured soldiers in Afghanistan were the same techniques they used to put my arms and legs back together."). As a result, she is mostly made out of metal. "I don't go off at the airport, though, which I'm really disappointed about."

The accident put a lot of things into perspective. "There's always somebody worse off than you," says Stuart, "and I think that's what we discovered in hospital. She was that drugged up, and she was saying to me 'I'm making friends on this ward and they're disappearing.' People would die, and she'd be asking for them."

For Dawn, the crash also hardened her concern for others. "If it's not life-threatening, I don't care!" she laughs. "I've no sympathy. If Stuart's ill I just close the door, and say, 'Come out when you're better'. I hate it when people rattle on about things that aren't major; I can't sympathise.

"I was with a lot of military patients, seventeen year-old lads back from Afghanistan. That gave me a lot of perspective. If you're healthy, that's the most important thing. If you've got that, then you can deal with pretty much anything."

Three years after the crash – and after doctors had given her the all clear – Dawn and Stuart underwent their first round of IVF. It worked first time, and scans revealed that they were pregnant with twins. "We were made up," says Dawn, "thinking this is how it is, this is easy. I was filling in my pregnancy journal and everything."

At about fourteen weeks, though, Dawn suffered a miscarriage and lost one of her twins. The other, thankfully, was fine; and Dawn and Stuart, although devastated, clung onto the fact that they still had one baby.

However, at twenty-two weeks, Dawn began feeling odd. A scan revealed that she was losing amniotic fluid, but doctors could not determine why. She spent a month in hospital undergoing tests and observations. "Then, during one of the Doppler scans one morning, there was no heartbeat," she recalls, sadly. "That was it. It was over."

Throughout her time in hospital, Dawn was battling infections; without a spleen, which had been removed after the crash, she suffered from a poor immune system. It later transpired that she had an infection of the placenta, which eventually cut off blood supply to her baby. Despite the best efforts of the doctors, the infection could not be pinpointed in time. "The hospital staff did all they could," says Dawn. "They were fantastic."

Stuart found that he and Dawn were not alone in being unaware as to the full extent of risks associated with pregnancy. "I've got a friend who recently lost a baby; they found out at the twelve-week scan," he explains. "He said to me 'I'm so naïve about all the stuff that goes on with pregnancy. I just thought it was a case of 'wham, bam, thank you ma'am', and there's the baby."

Lydia was born naturally, and stayed with Dawn and Stuart in the hospital. They refused a post-mortem, knowing that in roughly half of all cases the results come back inconclusive. "My concern was that if it comes back with nothing, where does that leave you?" says Dawn. "It can make people blame themselves."

Despite knowing what caused Lydia's death, Dawn still held herself accountable. "I didn't leave the house for a month. I tried to revisit everything I'd done, everywhere I'd been, everything I'd eaten, every time I'd taken the dog for a walk and maybe gone a bit too far... I was trying to pinpoint one thing that had happened to cause this. Three years on, I've still not quite forgiven myself, but I'm getting there. My body failed."

Stuart told family and friends the bad news. "They were dumbstruck," he says. "It's not really happened to anyone close to us." Dawn's mother was deeply affected, the loss of Lydia bringing back memories of the death of her own child.

The words "there is no heartbeat", each one pounding like a hammer blow, were uttered on Friday 13th October. Lydia was born the next day, in the early hours of the morning. Dawn and Stuart went home in the evening of the same day, after spending precious time with their daughter. Whilst in hospital, Dawn refused to let the staff take away her morphine drip, instead pressing the button to release more into her system: "It numbs the emotions. I didn't want to come back out into the real world; I was protected in that little room."

Stuart found the confined nature of the room claustrophobic. "Having cried that much, I just had to get out, and I know it may have been selfish to want to leave the hospital, but I didn't want to see Dawn going through any more. It was the worst day of my life, and I didn't want to make it go on any longer.

"I wanted to go, but I didn't want to leave Lydia. She was so beautiful: 1lb 1oz, blonde hair."

Dawn and Stuart had to register their daughter's birth and death on the same day, sat in a waiting room surrounded by newborns. "It's so wrong, and so cruel," says Dawn. "Stuart had to go to the receptionist and say: 'You either get us in or get us out of here, because she can't sit here with these newborns any more.'"

Lydia was brought home on the morning of her funeral. Stuart and Dawn had only just moved into their new house; their neighbours' first sense of what had happened was when a hearse pulled up outside and a white coffin was carried from the front door. Inside were a few items placed there by family, including an out-of-focus holiday photograph where Dawn and Stuart smile happily through sunburn.

The funeral was held at Sutton crematory; a small affair, attended only by family. At the moment, Lydia's ashes are back home; Dawn and Stuart continue to look for the perfect place to scatter them. "I'm waiting for the place to find me," says Dawn. "I'd like somewhere I can go with the twins, when they're old enough."

Stuart had to return to work shortly after the funeral; but for Dawn, remaining at home, life stopped. "I didn't work, so I had nothing else to do. That was what I was going to be: I was going to be a full-time mum, and I was going to be the best mum; going to all these groups, and do baby massage, and everything."

Stuart would often come home to find his wife crying over photographs of their daughter. At the time, the sorrow was overwhelming, but looking back, Dawn realises that being cocooned in her house gave her time to grieve. She was also fortunate enough to have a strong group of friends who provided her with encouragement and support. Now she can pass on her advice and experiences to others in the same situation, recognising the emotions that they feel. "I say to them 'It doesn't matter if it takes you a year before you can go out and see a pregnant woman and not want to hit her, it's OK.'"

Did Dawn harbour a lot of anger and resentment following Lydia's death? "I was quite confused as to why it had happened to me after everything else we'd gone through. I found myself getting wound up easily: for example, if I was in a supermarket and a parent was getting really stressed because their kid was having a tantrum, I was thinking 'Bad parents; they don't deserve to have children', and I'd give them dirty looks."

In the months following her loss, Dawn could only react with bitterness when family members shared the good news that they were expecting a baby. "I had a lot of anger," she recalls. "It took about eighteen months before it began to subside."

For Stuart, whose days were taken up with work, grieving was very much an intermittent process, a few moments stolen here and there. "Something would spark it off," he says. "I remember not grieving for months when my nan died, and then driving home from a shop one day I just pulled over in the car, and the sorrow hit me. It was the same with Lydia.

"The photo haunts me, of the holiday. Although it was a happy time, it haunts me, and so does the image of Lydia's face. That'll never leave."

Dawn and Stuart found that those who had experience of losing a child knew what to say to them, but some people avoided the subject altogether. "Quite a few people didn't know what to say, so they didn't say anything, and that's hard," explains Dawn. "I wanted her acknowledged. I didn't always want to talk about it, but I wanted them to acknowledge what was going on, because to me the world had stopped. I couldn't get my head around people going out to work. I really struggled with everyone carrying on. Who cares what the weather's like?"

*

Four months after Lydia's death, Dawn and Stuart underwent another round of IVF. In total, they have had seven courses of

IVF: "The bank manager isn't very happy with us," Dawn says, with a slight grin.

After the sixth course of IVF failed, Dawn and Stuart came across an article about Dr Taranissi, a fertility expert in London who has been the subject of some controversy throughout his professional life. However, he is highly rated within fertility websites; and so they booked an appointment to see him. He did some tests, and told them to come back in seven months, instructing them to go on holiday to clear their minds, gain some perspective, and be completely sure that they wanted to undergo another course of IVF.

Dawn and Stuart duly obliged, travelling to the Maldives for three weeks; a holiday Dawn describes as 'heaven'. "As a couple, we needed it." she states. "I was so relaxed I couldn't even be bothered to read."

But their hearts were still set on IVF. For Stuart, though, this would be their final attempt. "I was getting to the point where I thought I was going to have to say something. I thought 'if this doesn't work, it's just like setting money on fire.'"

Treatment under the guidance of Dr Taranassi began, and Dawn moved to London for three weeks. She was given tests and placed on a strict diet: two pints of full fat milk a day ("I can't stand milk"), three litres of water a day ("You were drinking so much water I can't believe you didn't drown"), and boiled eggs – alongside a handful of drugs which had to be picked up from the pharmacy every day.

Then came the day of 'retrieval', when Stuart would provide his sperm sample in order to fertilise Dawn's ova. That, in itself, was quite an ordeal.

"They showed me the little boy's room, and told me to do

my business," laughs Stuart. "About an hour and a half later, the nurse came up to me and said 'How do you feel about going again?' Apparently I had a blockage; so I had to go back to the room, past all these people who all know what I'm there for. You go in, come back out, everyone's staring at you, and you're like: 'Alright there?'

"An hour and a half later, she asked me to go *again*. I said 'There's nothing there', but went back for a second humiliation anyway. Then, an hour and a half later, she told me that it'd have to be surgery. I've never had an operation in my life, and I had to wait all day because I'd had a full English breakfast so they couldn't operate, and then in the evening I went into theatre. Afterwards, Mr Taranissi came running up to me and yelled 'We have sperm!', and ran back downstairs! We had to leave afterwards, both of us walking like John Wayne, into a taxi."

A few weeks – and several tests – later, Dawn discovered that she was pregnant with twins. She cried. Were they tears of joy or sadness? "I was scared. It was a déjà vu kind of moment. They'd put two embryos in, but I didn't think I was going to get one."

Dawn's pregnancy, in general, went well – bar a few setbacks where she suffered from bleeding. At one point, at around eighteen weeks, she was in hospital for seven days. "They said with that much blood, it was unlikely that everything was OK," she says, "but fortunately both babies were fine."

Due to Dawn's age (a shade over forty) and her history, she was monitored very closely. A consultant booked her in for a cervical stitch at fourteen weeks, after Dawn was diagnosed with an incompetent cervix: a crucial factor, perhaps, in the loss of Lydia. Then she was given scans every two weeks until around twenty-nine weeks pregnant, after which she was scanned in hospital every two or three days. Both babies were breech, but there was no major cause for concern. The hospital staff, Dawn says, were "better than good."

She was booked in for a Caesarean section at thirty-seven weeks, but was taken into hospital at thirty-six weeks after feeling unwell. The doctors took her blood pressure and decided to keep her in overnight. At two or three o'clock in the morning, Dawn awoke to a searing pain in her back. "I've never felt anything like it before," she remembers, "I actually screamed out."

Believing Dawn to be in labour, the midwives rushed her into a delivery suite. Further tests, however, found that she was suffering from an acute kidney infection, which had easily overcome her weak immune system. A few hours later, and hooked up to a drip, Dawn felt much better.

A midwife came round to do a routine internal examination, and left the room. Barely a minute later, she re-entered putting a theatre gown on, and threw another gown at Stuart. "Get that on, these babies need to be born now," she said. One of the twin's feet was protruding from Dawn's cervix.

Emelia and Jenson were delivered by Caesarean section, and both were handed straight to Dawn. "It was wonderful," she recalls, with a smile. "But even then, I didn't believe I was coming home with two babies. All through my pregnancy I was daydreaming about what it'd be like to have twins, or what it'd be like to have a baby, but I never really believed it was going to happen; I never let myself believe. I constantly thought something was going to go wrong."

It took Dawn a month to fully bond with her babies. "I never resented them or neglected them, but for me parenting was a process. I was constantly thinking 'I've got to do the bottle, I've got to feed that one, I've got to write down how many ounces they've had.'

"But then I remember going into the nursery one day and just sitting and watching them, smiling in total disbelief. When you've lost a baby, I don't think you allow yourself to enjoy pregnancy. My babies missed out on bonding during pregnancy, because I wouldn't allow it."

Dawn and Stuart have talked about releasing balloons on the anniversary of Lydia's birth, but instead find that they just shut down for the day, in silent remembrance of their daughter. They talk about Lydia in front of the twins, but at the moment they are too young to grasp what happened.

"I want them to know that they had a big sister, but I don't want it to overshadow them," explains Dawn. "I want them to be aware, but not affected by it. She'll always be a part of our life. They don't need to know the gory bits, they just need to know there's a little angel or a little star somewhere."

Dawn and Stuart have travelled a long and rough road to become parents, and have overcome many obstacles along the way. They have their twins, but will never forget Lydia.

But, after years of waiting, they have finally found their daughter's resting place: buried lovingly alongside the ashes of Dawn's mother, who passed away in August 2012.

Beautiful Lydia

Adapted from a poem found on the Sands forum,
and read at Lydia's funeral in remembrance of her and her sibling

You came to us to dry our tears,
To ease the pain of the last few years.
Beautiful Lydia we did not know
Our time together would be so short, before you had to go.

All we can do is ask ourselves 'why'
Our beautiful Lydia had to die?

There is no limit to love, no limit to pain,
Beautiful Lydia we will see you again.
And when that time comes
We know you'll be there
To open the gates and say "mommy & daddy are here".

This time the tears will be of joy and not pain,
Along with your twin we can be a family again.
We can hold you, kiss you
And surround you with love,
And finally forget that sad day you were taken from us.

Beautiful babies, we want you to know that mommy & daddy
love you both so.

Stay warm, our little darlings.
Love mommy & daddy
XXXXX

Rebecca

Carolyn Bray and her husband, Grev, first decided that they were 'boyfriend and girlfriend' whilst sat in a plane on a runway at Gatwick Airport. She had been going through a difficult patch in her life; he was planning a visit to see his brother in Nebraska, and suggested that Carolyn accompanied him to get away from it all. They had been friends for years, after having met through mutual friends at a local pub, but as they waited for take-off they made the decision to become an item. "I left my job, cashed in my cheques at the Post Office and threw caution to the wind!" laughs Carolyn.

Bizarrely, although Carolyn cannot remember how Grev proposed – although she knows he did so more than once – she remembers the date clearly: April 6th. Their wedding day was held in October 1995 at St Thomas' Church in Boston.

"All we were bothered about was getting married," remembers Carolyn. "The sun shone, we had all the people there that we wanted. I wore a white meringue dress – which was a little limp – and we had confetti, photos, a meal, a cake... one of my fondest memories has to be of my grandma and her best friend Betty. They put glitter in the vents of Grev's car, and when we left for our honeymoon he turned the heaters on we got covered in glitter!"

Carolyn, who was adopted as a child, had always dreamed of

having a large family of her own, and a year after she and Grev were married they decided to start thinking about having children. It was taking a while for that elusive positive pregnancy test, and after a few months of trying Carolyn began suffering from a mystery illness which caused her to lose weight rapidly. Hospital staff carried out a scan in an attempt to find the cause of her ill health; and, to everyone's surprise, the scan revealed that Carolyn and Grev were set to become parents.

"I'd not given it much thought, and so it was a bit of a shock to find out that way!" says Carolyn. "I ended up telling Grev in the car park of the hospital. He was chuffed to bits and rang his mother, brother and best mate there and then!"

Carolyn describes the pregnancy itself as "uneventful", and continued to work until going on maternity leave six weeks before her due date. "I continued my life as I knew it without any difficulties. I remember carrying a tumble-dryer up the stairs on my due date! I suffered really bad indigestion during the end of my pregnancy, which was so bad at night I had to sleep sitting up. I'm not very big, and so I resembled a Weeble for a long time!"

In contrast to Carolyn's pregnancy, the birth of her and Grev's first child was a stressful time. After two attempts to induce labour (Carolyn was two weeks overdue), a dose of Pethidine, an assisted forceps delivery, and a major episiotomy – "which had a huge impact on me for many years to come" – their son Matt was born just before midnight on 20th March 1998.

Now in his early teens, Matt has grown to be Carolyn and Grev's "chocolate éclair": tough on the outside, but soft centred. When asked about his childhood, Carolyn reels off a list of funny stories, including a memorable event in their garden.

"Matt was toilet training, and we were sat outside on a warm day. Matt was just toddling around in a t-shirt, and as he was playing he started doing a number two. Obviously the sensation caused him to stop playing and turn around to see what was happening, at which point he saw a "brown snake chasing him" and proceeded to run around the garden. Grev and I could do nothing but howl with laughter – to this day I still find myself laughing out loud at it!"

It was four years before Carolyn – who admits to finding motherhood difficult, and remarks that "sleep deprivation is the worst form of torture" – fell pregnant again. The pregnancy itself began smoothly, as it did with Matt: "I took it very much for granted. Grandma – one of the 'Glitter Grannies' at our wedding – died in the January, and the day of the funeral was the first time I felt a kick."

At thirty-eight weeks pregnancy, and during a routine check-up, the midwife expressed concern at the size of Carolyn's baby, and referred her for an ultrasound to be carried out six days later. That evening, though, a concerned Carolyn rang the labour ward of her local hospital and asked to be checked over.

"I was met with reluctance," recalls Carolyn, "and ended up saying that I'd not felt my baby move. At this time, this was a lie – I just wanted some reassurance. They agreed to see me, and strapped me up to a heart monitor. The printout looked to me to be very erratic, but the midwife said it was fine, and so we went home."

A few days later, Matt and Carolyn returned home from bargain-hunting at a car boot sale when she experienced severe tightening. Putting it down to spending the day on her feet, Carolyn had a bath to try and alleviate the pain. It didn't work.

"I rang the ward and explained the succession of events and

how I felt. The lady on the other end of the phone asked some questions and then said in a very firm voice that I needed to come in soon."

Carolyn and Grev dropped Matt off at a friend's house and drove the fifteen minutes to hospital, by which time Carolyn was in a lot of pain. Met by the lady she had spoken to on the phone, who never left their sides, they were ushered into a room where a heart monitor revealed nothing but silence. Blaming faulty equipment, the hospital staff fetched a different monitor; but again, there was nothing, save the "haunting loud echo of silence", as Carolyn describes it.

"I turned to Grev and said that it had gone wrong; he said it was fine, and not to worry. I was taken for an ultrasound – it was mid-afternoon on a Tuesday, and the place was in darkness. They scanned me, and then said the words 'I'm sorry, there is no heartbeat. Your baby is dead.' The midwife was stood at the bottom of the bed and squeezed my feet; all I could think was that my feet would smell."

Carolyn had suffered a full placental abruption, and because she had been bleeding internally for some time her organs were beginning to fail. She deteriorated rapidly, and so she was induced whilst being given a cocktail of drugs and worked on for eight hours.

"I was barely aware of anything," says Carolyn, "but it must have been the longest eight hours of Grev's life. He ended up having to give instructions to me as his was the only voice I would respond to. Our baby girl Rebecca was born silently at 11.08pm. Being told that the baby you thought was going to be a boy was in fact a girl sent me reeling; it never occurred to me that we'd have a girl. I thought it was all just a dream, and that I would wake up soon."

The hospital staff – who Carolyn describes as "faultless" – took a few photographs of Rebecca once Carolyn was stable. At the time, they seemed unimportant, but today Carolyn is grateful that they were taken, even if there were just a small handful. "Not many were taken, which has to be my biggest regret."

Carolyn required a blood transfusion, and was ill for some time. In order to protect Matt from the experience of seeing his mother so unwell, she and Grev decided not to let him visit the hospital: something which they now regret, as Matt has never seen his baby sister.

"The days in hospital are a complete blur," recalls Carolyn. "I came out of hospital on 7th June, and it was Grev's birthday the next day. The mix of 'Happy Birthday' and 'With Sympathy' cards was surreal. We punished ourselves, wondering what we had done which was so bad that we had to lose our daughter."

Rebecca was cremated a week later, following a service attended only by a small number of people. 'The Dance' by Garth Brooks was played, and yellow roses were placed by a headstone in the local cemetery. Rebecca wore a christening bangle – one of two; the other one can be found on the arm of a teddy bear bought by her great uncle in the days following her funeral.

"I regret not taking more photos," says Carolyn, "not having photos of Rebecca and her daddy, not seeing her naked, not seeing her feet, not spending enough time holding and taking in every part of her, and not realising or fully comprehending the importance of that time together."

The weeks which followed are a haze in the minds of Carolyn and Grev. Without support or advice from those who had experienced a similar tragedy, they found themselves in a permanent daze. Matt became the reason for them to get out of bed; everywhere they turned, they were faced with reminders of Rebecca. Carolyn remembers standing in the playground of Matt's school, surrounded by people but feeling incredibly lonely.

"Rebecca had been born during the school half term, and myself and another mum had joked about who would have their baby first," she remembers. "She won. Standing in the playground pushing no pram whilst all the other mums stood around hers is, to this day, the most devastating feeling. I can hardly explain the pain, that pain which I can still feel today."

Many friendships were lost in the time following Rebecca's death; not because of anger or animosity, but a drifting apart caused by not knowing what to say. "When something so huge happens, you end up questioning everything, including friendships. The majority didn't know what to do, and some we've never spoken to since it happened.

"Some people were helpful, some were not. I had every cliché thrown at me: one friend sat with me not six weeks afterwards and suggested it was about time I got on with my life… I'll never forget that. I figured that was what everyone thought, and so I just got on with things and buried everything."

Fortunately, though, many true friends were at hand to offer words of advice and support. "The one thing I'll never forget is a friend telling me that 'You never get over something like this, you just learn to live with it'. Grev's best friend and his wife bought a beautiful oak tree in Rebecca's memory, and it was planted in the cemetery. Every single year on her birthday they send us a single yellow rose. A friend's son came around nearly every Thursday to see how we were doing, and to this day I've never forgotten that. Another friend allowed me to talk, and would talk with me too; she asked about things, and she was the only person to acknowledge how awful, horrendous and life-changing this had been."

A close friend likened Carolyn to a blue vase on a mantelpiece, smashed to pieces and lovingly glued back together. From a distance, it looked complete; but upon closer inspection, the cracks were obvious. On the outside, it looked functional, but it would never hold water again.

Carolyn spent a lot of time online after losing Rebecca, talking to parents in the same situation and making good friends. She and Grev were amazed to discover that a great number of people who they had known for a long time had also had similar experiences. "Baby death is such a taboo subject, and unspoken of."

Matt provided Carolyn and Grev with chinks of light during their darkest days; not least when he confronted a woman who commented on the age gap between him and Carolyn's third child, James. "It was a very proud 'mummy moment'," she smiles, "when Matt turned round and said that he had a sister but that she was in Heaven. The woman was beside herself."

*

Soon after Rebecca's death, and experiencing an "intense longing" to be pregnant, Carolyn and Grev discovered that they were expecting their third child; news that was met with "fear, disbelief and shock". Friends and family considered the pregnancy to be the 'sticking plaster' for the bereaved parents' grief: it was going to be okay this time. Carolyn, however, had a different view: "The pregnancy was, in my opinion, horrific. It was like holding my breath for nine months.

"I was very pragmatic during this pregnancy: I just went with 'what will be, will be'. I guess it was a coping mechanism. I couldn't accept that there would be a positive outcome; but this time, unlike the previous two, I had to find out the sex of our baby."

This in itself brought challenges: if it was a girl, it would be a daily reminder of Rebecca, and what she would have looked like, or acted like. If it was a boy, then Carolyn would never experience the mother-daughter relationship she longed for, as she and Grev had agreed that this would be their third and last child. At the twenty-week scan they discovered they were having a boy: James.

Every day of pregnancy, says Carolyn, felt like a week. Most of the time, it was déjà-vu, very cruel and emotionally exhausting. Hospital staff, the majority of whom were aware of Carolyn and Grev's previous loss, provided scans and check-ups every fortnight, then every week, as the due date drew ever closer. Carolyn and Grev wrote a birth plan which extended to three pages: the first two entitled 'If it goes wrong', and a few lines on the third which explained their wishes if childbirth was going well. "We didn't need any more than that," says Carolyn. "We'd have the rest of our lives to fill that page."

Carolyn was induced at thirty-eight weeks, in the same room in which she gave birth to Rebecca – a specific request. The same midwife who looked after Carolyn and Grev after the loss of their daughter was present. The birth was a very surreal experience for all involved.

"Between gulps of gas and air I was flitting between reliving Rebecca's birth and experiencing James'," explains Carolyn. "Grev had no idea; the midwife eventually cottoned on to what was happening. I would cry and refer to Rebecca as the drugs started to work, and then when they wore off I was normal again, talking coherently as if nothing was untoward."

James was born at 5pm, weighing just two ounces more than Rebecca. Carolyn made the midwife clean his eyes and open them, just so that she could see he was awake.

Carolyn describes the first three weeks of motherhood as "pure, wonderful, indescribable pleasure" – but, on her birthday just three weeks after James was born, their lives were shattered again: James had Cystic Fibrosis.

"I had to tell Grev that night," recalls Carolyn. "To this day, it is the single most difficult thing I have ever had to do. To watch your husband, the father of your children, your best friend, disintegrate and sob 'I've already had to bury one child, I can't do that again' is indescribable. We had embarked upon a new chapter of our lives."

Losing Rebecca has changed Carolyn and Grev's lives forever. They describe losing a child as "the most horrific thing", and firmly believe that awareness of stillbirth should be greatly increased, and are dismayed at just how common it is. Carolyn has been involved with Sands for the last nine years, both in a voluntary capacity and as part of their fundraising team.

"There is nothing you can say to someone in the first few days, weeks months or even years which will make much of a difference," she says. "You will never believe that you will get through, and that life will not be an excruciatingly painful black hole, but it will get better. You will stop feeling guilty when you laugh, and you will find yourself enjoying life again. You will never forget your precious child, and they will always be a part of your life and shape the person you are to become. Only ever do what is right for you, and only you."

Every year, on Rebecca's birthday, Carolyn and Grev take the day off work and spend it somewhere new, somewhere they have never been before, to create a new memory that they can dedicate to their daughter. Then, they visit Rebecca's headstone and put up cards, balloons and flowers.

"I don't have a particular treasured memory of Rebecca," says Carolyn when asked, "but what I do believe she gave us was a gift; a gift to find true friends. We are not meant to outlive our children. I'm far more patient and tolerant, empathetic and accepting nowadays. I'm not the person I was prior to that day ten years ago; that Carolyn died too. We are a family of five: it's just one of us is not on earth."

The Dance', by Garth Brooks

Played at Rebecca's funeral

Looking back on the memory of
The dance we shared 'neath the stars alone
For a moment all the world was right
How could I have known that you'd ever say goodbye

And now I'm glad I didn't know
The way it all would end the way it all would go
Our lives are better left to chance
I could have missed the pain
But I'd have had to miss the dance

Holding you I held everything
For a moment wasn't I a king
But if I'd only known how the king would fall
Hey, who's to say you know I might have chanced it all

And now I'm glad I didn't know
The way it all would end the way it all would go
Our lives are better left to chance
I could have missed the pain
But I'd of had to miss the dance

Yes, my life is better left to chance
I could have missed the pain
But I'd have had to miss the dance.

Baby Dewberry

It was 2001 when Joanne Dewberry met her husband, David, in the heat of the Turkish sun, where they both worked for a holiday company: Joanne worked in the Kid's Club, and David was a lifeguard.

Ten years later they are still going strong, and have three children – Charlie, Megan and Olive – but, as in the case of so many parents, they have had to endure heartache to get to where they are today.

When Joanne discovered that she was pregnant for the first time, she couldn't wait to tell David. "I told him over the phone," she says, "I was so excited!"

However, pregnancy was not kind to Joanne, and left her feeling ill. "I was really sick," she recalls. "My skin was awful, my hair was super-greasy and I felt shocking." Whilst apprehensive about how she would cope with this level of illness, Joanne's intuition told her that something was not quite right. Then, the night before her twelve-week scan, she had a small bleed.

Panicked, she called the midwife, who told her that slight bleeding was common. The twelve-week scan came, during which the sonographer asked if Joanne minded having an internal examination. "I'd never been pregnant before, so I wasn't really sure what to think."

Joanne agreed, and during the internal examination the

bleeding began again. Then the news was broken that her womb held a placenta – but no baby. "We were taken into another room and offered a drink," remembers Joanne. "And someone came and explained to us what was happening. This is all a bit blurry, as I was mortified."

Pieces of the jigsaw were put into place. Joanne's placenta was the right size for twelve weeks, but the medical staff believed that the baby had died a few weeks earlier and had been engulfed by the placenta – which, Joanne believes, was exhibited in her extreme morning sickness.

Over the following two days Joanne suffered the loss of several large clots, and went into hospital to be scanned again. The scan showed that her placenta had continued to grow, but that the lining of the womb was shedding. The next day, a Tuesday, Joanne was admitted to hospital and given a dilation and curettage under general anaesthetic. The operation went well, and Joanne was released later that day.

Although Joanne was healing physically, mentally the wounds were still open. "I was devastated," she says, sadly. "Having never been pregnant before, or even having a near-miss situation, I was worried that I wouldn't be able to have children."

Joanne found herself in limbo. At the time, she ran a pre-school, so found herself surrounded by children every day. Meanwhile, beneath a happy exterior, she mourned the loss of her own child, and longed to become a mother.

She and David were both grieving, but coped by not talking about their feelings. Joanne found her family to be wonderfully supportive – as were the hospital staff, who offered her and David counselling.

After losing a child, many people say things in an attempt to

122

provide support. For Joanne, one remark hit home. "Someone said to me that there are normally issues with the baby, and miscarriage is your body's way of dealing with this. After having three healthy children, I'm inclined to believe that my first pregnancy was not meant to be, and was unhealthy."

*

Joanne, by her own admission, became obsessed by getting pregnant again; and, a year later, her wish was granted. Upon seeing the little blue cross, her first emotion was apprehension, followed closely by worry. This persisted until she had her twelve-week scan.

Joanne suffered none of the sickness that was so prevalent previously, and describes the pregnancy as "brilliant". Labour, however, was an altogether more difficult experience. Joanne experienced contractions on her due date, and went into hospital at 11pm. Twelve hours later, she was still just four centimetres dilated.

"My waters had been broken, and still nothing was really happening," she recalls. "I was moved onto a ward and hooked up to monitors and machines, which pumped me full of drugs; Pethidine for the pain, and hormones to kick-start labour."

After a while, her baby – a boy, who she and David had named Charlie – had become stuck and unresponsive. A consultant entered and set out the options: either a ventouse delivery, or a Caesarean section. Adamant that she did not want a C-section – "I was shouting" – the hospital staff set to work with the ventouse.

Fortunately, it worked, and at 4.40pm Charlie arrived. His

123

head was slightly cone-shaped – a characteristic of a ventouse delivery – and an exhausted Joanne held her son, experiencing what she described as "the best feeling ever".

Joanne and David went on to have two more children, Megan and Olive. Their birth stories were a stark contrast to that of Charlie: both were delivered with the aid of gas and air, and in much quicker times. "With Charlie I really didn't know what to do," says Joanne, "but with the girls I knew exactly what to do, and I was in control of my body and what was happening." Three kids must be a handful, surely? Joanne laughs. "I must be crazy!"

Crazy, perhaps: but, even when her time was spent looking after a preschool full of children, as well as raising her own – she has since started her own business – Joanne will never forget her first child who never was. Shortly after discovering she had suffered a miscarriage, Joanne bought a teddy bear and named it Milo: "a name which we liked for a son". She took it into hospital for her operation, and later her two eldest children took it in turns to sleep with him.

Now, Milo sits in Olive's cot. As yet, none of Joanne's children are aware of his significance: but, to Joanne and David, the sight of the small teddy bear lying next to their baby will always be a poignant reminder of their first, lost child.

Abigail

By her own admission, Jo Ward is not the same woman David married. The experiences that they have tackled together has thickened her skin, made her more resilient, and – ultimately – changed her altogether.

"As much as I would like to go back to be the person I was, too much has happened in my life," she says. "I find it hard to open up, and talk about my feelings; I try to be Miss Independent."

Jo was pregnant when she walked down the aisle towards David, after having discovered five months previously that they were expecting a child. They had just returned from holiday, and David was over the moon at the news that he was to be a father. The news was slightly tempered, though, as Jo had suffered a miscarriage at ten weeks in a previous pregnancy. As such, the first few weeks after they found out they were expecting another were characterised by anxiety.

"I was very nervous in the early days," recalls Jo, "and just wanted to get to my twelve-week so-called 'safe' stage."

The 'safe' stage arrived, and Jo spent the rest of her pregnancy being the textbook expectant mother: no alcohol, a good diet, and excellent overall health. As the nine months drew nearer, she began to relax, thinking that if her daughter, Abigail, were to arrive early then she would be fine. Her due date came and went;

the day after, sensing something wasn't right, Jo and David went to hospital.

Jo was taken to triage on the delivery suite and attached to the monitors, where the midwives studied the equipment read-outs and decided to transfer her to another room. Jo could tell that the news was bad – "I knew our little girl had gone" – and that the staff were trying to buy more time until a more senior doctor could confirm what they suspected.

Eventually, Jo and David's fears were confirmed, and they were told to return to hospital the following morning so Jo could be induced. Instead of going home, they went to Jo's parents' house, where they broke the awful news to her family. "Abigail had touched so many people's lives, and seeing how upset people were before she was even born was so distressing."

Jo was induced in the morning as planned, and the hospital staff invited her to go home and wait for labour to start. Unable to face returning to a house full of baby clothes and toys, Jo and David shut themselves away in Room 11 – a small side room in the hospital that would be their home for the next two days. There, they sat and waited, asking themselves questions without answers: Why us? What had we done wrong?

Their talking helped to drown out the sound of other babies being born, which echoed down the hospital corridors "like a punishment". "David and I sat and supported one another during the hardest days of our lives, just sitting and waiting."

Eventually, labour began, and it progressed quickly. Jo requested a Caesarean section, which was refused: a decision which, in time, proved to be the right one. Jo recalls the story of Abigail's birth with a faint smile.

"At the time, I was extremely upset that I had to go through the whole birth, but now I am so glad that I did. I gave birth to my daughter as I had planned, and even though it was the darkest days of our lives it was an amazing experience that I will always share with my little girl."

Abigail was born – "perfect in every way" – and handed to David for him to cuddle. These moments with their daughter, the first time she was placed in their arms, are Jo's most treasured memories.

Aware that approximately half of all results come back inconclusive, and unable to face the notion that Abigail would be taken away, Jo and David refused a post-mortem. A few days later, the local crematorium was filled with family and friends, all wanting to pay their respects and show their love towards the little girl whom they had never met. At Jo and David's request, each guest wore something pink, and after the funeral a hundred pink balloons were released into the sky, decorated with personal messages.

Jo describes the following weeks as "a blur". "I don't know where I got the strength to carry on," she says. "David was my rock, and my family – especially my sister – were fantastic. They spent so much time with me, as they didn't want me to be on my own."

A few weeks after the funeral, David reluctantly returned to work, leaving Jo at home with nothing to focus on, no purpose. "My purpose was to be a mum," she explains, "and that had been snatched away from me."

What Jo found particularly difficult was that, in time, those around them would overcome their grief and return to normality. This left Jo in a state of limbo: unable to move on, but having to witness those around her continuing with their lives.

"I found that incredibly hard," she remembers. "I had lost my baby, but things carried on as normal, and I couldn't deal with that. It took me a long time to adjust and accept that life does carry on. David would remind me that Abigail would not want me to be so unhappy, and that I had to get up in the morning and carry on. The guilt I felt was enormous. If I could have swapped places with Abigail, I would have done."

Abigail would forever be a part of their lives, but Jo and David were keen for her never to be forgotten: and so, when David was home, they talked about Abigail, finding therapy in their conversation. Their loss strengthened their relationship, and they spent hours talking about how they felt, and the future; each person providing strength and encouragement to the other.

But there were times, naturally, when Jo and David both felt overwhelmed by their loss: especially when they saw friends with healthy, newborn babies. Jo speaks candidly about how she felt.

"A friend had her baby four days after I had Abigail. I couldn't bear to see her, or her baby; I was so jealous and hurt that everything was fine for her. It took me two years before I could face seeing her or her son, because it's a reminder of the exact stage that Abigail would have been at. It's not her fault that she had a healthy son, but I am not strong enough to deal with seeing them on a social basis, even now. I will be polite if I see them, but it breaks my heart."

Misplaced advice also hurt Jo as she attempted to pick up the pieces of her life. Someone close to her, meaning well, suggested that she scatter Abigail's ashes to help put her to rest. "It was said so matter-of-factly, with no real thought on how I might feel," says Jo. "I can't bear the thought of Abigail not being with me, and I will keep her ashes at home until the day I die."

The occasional throwaway comment aside, Jo found a lot of comfort in the words of others during the months after losing Abigail. The midwives who helped deliver her daughter have since become very close friends. One person said that Abigail was too precious for this world, which she found comforting. The majority of her strength, though, came from David and her family – although she summoned a lot of courage herself to find the will to continue.

"I needed a reason to carry on, and I knew that I would want to try for another baby straight away; not to replace Abigail, but to provide a brother or sister for her."

Jo and David also found another way to channel their grief, and turn their tragedy into something positive: they opened a bridal shop called Abigail's, and donate £17 to Sands for every dress sold.

*

A year passed, and Abigail's first birthday arrived. Keen to keep busy and distracted, Jo and David went on a short holiday: "I would have crumbled otherwise," she explains. The trip helped, but did not occupy Jo's mind as much as the notion of having another baby; for, by this point, she was five months pregnant.

"We were both ecstatic when we found out," recalls Jo, "but I was extremely nervous. We told our parents straight away, whereas with Abigail we waited until three months – but we needed that extra support."

The extra support was provided by the bucketful; but Jo became very introvert during her pregnancy, gripped with worry that she could lose another child. "I was worried that I had done something wrong to cause Abigail's stillbirth, and thought that if I did nothing during the pregnancy, I would be giving my child the best possible chance of survival."

And so, keen to protect her unborn child, Jo retreated into herself for the next nine months; an action which put a huge strain on her relationship with David. "The baby became my focus, and I couldn't deal with anything else," she says. "Looking back, I was an emotional wreck."

Being all too aware of the risks associated with pregnancy, Jo and David made numerous trips to the hospital to be monitored and checked. The care they received was incredible, and they were given "first-class treatment", made available in part thanks to the friendships they had cultivated following the loss of Abigail.

At thirty-seven weeks, keen to have a different birth experience, Jo underwent an elective Caesarean section. "It was a weird feeling, walking down to theatre knowing that in thirty minutes I would have a baby."

Everything went well, and a son – Reuben – was born. At fifteen months old, he is still a little too young to know what happened to Abigail, but he often kisses photographs of her which are dotted on shelves and mantelpieces around the house. On Abigail's second birthday, Jo found the courage to return to the crematorium, where she left a cuddly toy and a balloon. Her family did the same, and – although a painful experience – Jo is resolute that this will happen each year on her daughter's birthday.

Abigail's memory lives on: not just in the hearts and minds of friends and family, but as a registered charity. Abigail's Footsteps has raised over £15,000 for Sands through a number of events, including a parachute jump and a charity ball, which will become an annual occurrence. In the future, Jo hopes to set up a scholarship for bereavement midwives at her local hospital.

"The support that you receive can make such a difference to your future survival," she explains. "If we can save the life of one baby, then we have achieved our goal in saving other parents from the heartache we have been through. We know we can't change the world, but hopefully we can make a small difference."

Now expecting a third child, and a very different person than the one who walked down the aisle just a few years ago, Jo cherishes every moment she has with David and Reuben. "I now realise that I have no control over things and that, in some cases, you just have to get on with it and take each day as it comes. When you lose a baby, the world is a dark place; but, with time, it gets easier."

When people ask how many children Jo has, she says that she has two and another on the way. Abigail will forever be a part of her family, and has a permanent place in the hearts of Jo and David, as well as in friends and relatives. Jo's young niece and nephews often talk about Abigail, and wonder what she is doing in heaven. And, whenever they are given a balloon, they will always release it into the sky, in tribute and memory to the cousin they never knew, yet love so dearly.

Baby Purnell

It wasn't exactly love at first sight when a fourteen-year-old Abi Purnell first laid eyes on Sam – although, after nine years together, she can laugh about it now. "He used to swan on in, seventeen years old, with that 'I can go out clubbing' cockiness about him. I despised him!"

He was the friend of her sister's flatmate, and effortlessly wound Abi up by calling her 'bird' at any given opportunity. Still, he must have done something right, and, outside a Debenhams store after their first date – watching *Toy Story* at the local cinema – made the first move of what would turn out to be a lasting relationship.

Thankfully, any romance that may have been lacking on the first date was more than made up for when Sam proposed on a pier at sunset whilst on a holiday in Saint-Tropez, a memory at which Abi gushes. "It was beautiful and amazing!"

The wedding day was equally as memorable, and the happy couple were married in a seaside chapel in Lindos Rhodes under the hot Grecian sun. "All of our loved ones were there to share our day with," she recalls. "We had our wedding evening at a traditional Greek taverna, Greek food, fun music and lots of laughter, tears of joy, singing, dancing… and limbo!"

Abi and Sam had grand plans to move to Australia: but, a few days after booking their wedding venue, Abi discovered she was pregnant. "It was an unexpected and wonderful surprise," she says. "We weren't trying for a baby, but we always knew we wanted children."

Early pregnancy came with the textbook symptoms: breast pain, nausea, migraines and exhaustion – as well as vivid nightmares. Now and again Abi would sleepwalk, and at one point spent most of the night trying to catch imaginary falling boulders.

In her third trimester Abi was diagnosed with cholestasis, a liver condition which can increase the percentage of stillbirth by up to 15%. As is often the case in cholestasis sufferers, Abi was induced at thirty-nine weeks, which marked the beginning of a very long and exhausting labour.

"I felt intense pain after the first pessary," she recalls. "I was then told to wait six hours for the next pessary, which I found difficult as I was in so much pain. I kept telling the midwives I was in labour, to which they said I wouldn't be."

Once the second pessary had been administered, Abi started vomiting. Told by the midwives that it was simply a sign of being in labour, she was examined and found to be only one centimetre dilated. After nine hours of being on a hormone drip – "this only sped up the pain and vomiting" – she was no further dilated. Finally, at 2 o'clock in the morning – after Pethidine and an epidural – Abi's waters were broken and she was told that she could begin to push. Two hours later, and "one push away from a C-section", Sam and Abi's daughter, Ephie, was born.

Abi explains how such an unusual and pretty name was chosen. "Samuel and I found it difficult to choose or compromise on a name, and one evening we were looking through the baby name book. I asked him to pick a letter, and he chose 'E'. I randomly started reading out names, and read 'Ephie'. I instantly fell in love with it, and Samuel said, 'that's the one.' To double check, I asked him to pick a page number at random: he chose 99. The name 'Ephie' was on the same page!"

Now a bright, sweet-natured young girl – and "the biggest drama queen going" – Ephie keeps her mum on her toes. Abi laughs as she recalls one recent occasion of Ephie's unbridled confidence.

"The other morning I was getting ready to take her to nursery and popped my hair up in a bun. Ephie stopped playing with her cars, looked up at me and said, 'Are you wearing your hair up?' I replied, 'Yes.'

"'Disgusting,' she muttered. I asked, 'What's disgusting, darling?' Ephie carried on playing with her cars, and quite confidently said: 'You, Mummy, you look disgusting.' Little madam!"

A week before Ephie's first birthday, Abi discovered that she was pregnant with her second child. It came as a pleasant surprise: although Abi had her suspicions, she was not fully convinced that she was pregnant, and took a test simply for peace of mind. When a very faint line occurred, Sam dashed to Asda and bought another test. The result was positive.

Early pregnancy brought with it all the symptoms that Abi had previously suffered, including a small amount of bleeding. Having suffered from bleeds whilst pregnant with Ephie – which was blamed on stress – Abi contacted the local hospital to get an appointment for an early scan.

The day of the ultrasound arrived, and brought with it an element of excitement: "I thought, 'I get to see my baby early!'" recalls Abi – and, once laid on the bed with the sonographer's wand at her stomach, she was asked how far gone she was. Abi knew the date instantly, thanks to regularly checking fertility charts: seven and a half weeks.

It was then that Abi and Sam were told that the baby was showing up smaller than Abi's estimations would allow, and was the size of a five and a half week baby. They were advised to book another scan in a fortnight's time to check the progress of their baby, which – assuming everything was fine, and it was a simple mix-up of dates – Abi and Sam agreed to. Then, a nurse called them into a room.

"She sat us down and asked if we understood that I was likely to be miscarrying," Abi recalls. "We replied that we didn't, as we had not been informed that this could be the case. The nurse then said that it was very likely that I had miscarried, and that the scan in two weeks was to confirm this. We were absolutely devastated."

The scan a fortnight later confirmed that Abi had suffered a missed miscarriage. The baby could not be found, having been reabsorbed by her body. However, being a missed miscarriage, Abi continued to suffer pregnancy symptoms. She was given two options: take some pills to quicken the process, or wait for it to happen naturally. Abi refused both, opting for the dilation and curettage procedure.

The operation was carried out without any problems, and Abi's pregnancy symptoms ceased soon afterwards. The hospital staff were considerate and helpful, apologising for Abi's loss whenever they met. "It was sweet of them to be supportive, but at the same time I didn't want to be reminded every five minutes why I was there. I wanted it all out, and to move on."

Abi had a few days off work, "to get my feet back on the ground and get my head straight". In the two weeks between scans she and Sam had prepared themselves for bad news, and in doing so had already begun to deal with the grief a miscarriage brings before the dilation and curettage operation was carried out. However, they often found it difficult to come to terms with the loss of their second child. "We couldn't talk to one another," recalls Abi. "I would cry and say I was going to bed, and Sam would get angry."

The double pram that the excited parents had bought had to be rewrapped and sent back. In time, though, both Abi and Sam came to cope with their loss. "We returned to normal, back to work and back on with life," she explains. "We had our beautiful girl Ephie that we could focus on."

Neither Abi nor Sam wanted too much sympathy; instead, they were relieved to find that everyone treated them normally. Friends expressed their condolences, and then said no more. "We were lucky to have a healthy child," explains Abi. "Our loss happened for a reason, and it wasn't meant to be."

*

The distressing occurrences of the previous few weeks had not dampened Abi and Sam's resolve to fall pregnant, though; and, four weeks later, a small blue cross on a test once again faded into view.

"It was planned," says Abi, "but we didn't think we would fall pregnant that quickly. I was so happy! I felt like I wouldn't be lucky enough to become pregnant again."

Fully aware of how common miscarriages are, Abi approached pregnancy as she had done previously: being as positive as possible. "I still feared the worst, but didn't want to fret on what could happen. I would rather not worry about the doom and gloom."

Suffering from the same pregnancy symptoms, Abi was once again diagnosed with cholestasis, and induced at thirty-eight and a half weeks. This time, labour happened much more quickly: after having the first pessary at midnight, Abi found herself in the throes of childbirth only seven hours later after dilating from five to ten centimetres in a matter of minutes.

"At one point they thought I was going to give birth in the corridor!" she exclaims. "My recorded labour was one hour and forty minutes... unbelievable!"

As there was only one midwife available at the time, Sam warmed and cleaned his baby son with the help of his mother-in-law, who had travelled to Abi's bedside for moral support. They named their baby boy Sennan, after a village near Land's End that they had fallen in love with during a family holiday. Concerned about his temperature, the hospital staff transferred him to the special care ward, from which he returned forty-five minutes later "looking a bit more pink and wrapped up in layers!"

Abi and Sam's loss has provided them with the opportunity to change their perspective on life. They both feel that there should be more awareness of miscarriage, and how common it is, but are resolute to focus on what they have.

"We are very lucky to have a '2.4 family'," says Abi. "It does make you think how lucky you are, and how some people are not fortunate enough to have just one healthy child."

Now and again, Abi will wonder what sex her lost baby would have been; but, as she describes it, "I lift my head up and focus on what I have. You have to pick up and try again. No-one wants to see you sad."

Freddie

It was five years after the birth of their fourth daughter when Merry and Max Raymond decided to try for another child. It was about eight months, though, before they successfully fell pregnant; surprising, as with each of Merry's four daughters she had conceived instantly.

Both Max and Merry were delighted; however, six weeks into the pregnancy, Merry suffered from bleeding. "I had enough to make me think that it was all over," she recalls. Fortunately, a blood test and subsequent scan showed that there was a baby, but that it was smaller than Merry thought likely. The doctors also suspected that Max and Merry's child had once been a twin, but that the second baby had been lost. Merry is remarkably honest about how she felt at the time.

"Rather glibly, I thought it was probably better there were not going to be two," she says, "but I was worried by how small that tiny thing with a heartbeat was. I put it out of my head."

Unfortunately, the blood test had collapsed Merry's vein onto a nerve in her arm, and she was in agony. Expecting to lose her baby, she did not protest when a doctor prescribed codeine for the pain. A few days later, perhaps triggered by the painkillers, Merry had a nightmare that she was looking at a baby who wouldn't open his eyes; a dream that would recur once more during her pregnancy.

The pregnancy itself was a nervous time for Merry – a marked contrast to her previous four pregnancies, during which she had happily written about her experiences. With her fifth, Merry was relentlessly anxious, tense during every test or scan. During the early weeks she told only a few close friends that she was pregnant. Nothing could calm her: "I just assumed something was going to go wrong."

This feeling of dread persisted, and manifested itself in unusual and incredibly unsettling ways. Three months into her pregnancy, Merry read about the death of a friend's daughter, who tragically died at just six hours old.

"I read a line about her children on the first night of knowing their baby sister had died, and my heart just sank," she remembers. "I thought: 'This is going to happen to us'. I remember the moment so clearly. It was just… I can't explain it: a moment where the future felt like it rushed in at me."

By this time, Merry's friends had become accustomed to her worry, and – although supportive – were "definitely rolling their eyes at me." Because of this, they were not told of her bizarre thoughts and sense of foreboding.

Ever since the twelve-week scan, Merry was convinced that she would be having a boy: and, eight weeks later, her suspicions were confirmed. After four daughters, it seemed they would indeed have a son. Merry recalls their reaction to the news.

"We'd never wanted one, and yet suddenly it seemed like an exciting idea. Max took a while to come round to it, but in the end he really fell in love with the idea. I was thrilled, but nervous, and was increasingly having very disconnected moments of thinking 'What have I done?' which didn't make any sense, because I had been quite literally desperate for a baby for three years."

Merry's feelings of dread evolved into an ongoing feeling that she was lying to herself about being pregnant. She found it almost impossible to visualise being in hospital and giving birth, and describes "feeling stupid" when buying breast pads and baby outfits. Her friend demonstrated how to wrap a sling, and Merry couldn't help but wonder why she was bothering. She and Max bought a feeding cushion, which – to Merry – seemed a pointless task.

"I felt as if I had told a huge lie, and very soon I was going to get found out," explains Merry. "I felt like Mary Tudor with her phantom pregnancies. I never, ever felt like I was going to have a baby."

At around seven months, Merry noticed that her baby was behaving strangely. If she lay on her left side, he would get fretful and move a lot. "I described it to Max as being as if he scrabbled away from that side of me, and wondered out loud if perhaps the baby had his cord around his back and didn't like the feeling of lying on it somehow."

Although her baby moved well and often, Merry's bump was noticeably small for the stage she was at; but, although concerned, she did not panic. In hindsight, she and Max both recognise that she was unusually calm, almost fatalist. "I barely shouted, ranted, wailed or stropped," she recalls, "and frankly, that's not normal!"

Bizarrely, Merry took up knitting, despite having rarely done so before. "It was incredibly important to me that this baby have something special that was just his, and I knitted squares and squares of stitches. I didn't do anything else; we didn't bring the cot down, I didn't nest, I didn't get nappies or clothes out. But I did knit, and I know it sounds ridiculous but with every square I knitted I thought about whether this blanket would be a shroud. I couldn't shake the idea of it."

Having kept her feelings to herself for the majority of her pregnancy, Merry finally opened up to Shona, her doula, although she does not really remember doing so. Later, though, Shona would tell Merry that during the early stages of labour she was noticeably less negative than she had been previously.

A few days after speaking to Shona, whilst with her husband, Merry had what she describes as a "hormonal weeping fit".

"I said to Max that I wanted him out, that he doesn't feel safe in there any more, and I want him out where I can look after him in my arms or let someone look after him if he is sick."

Merry's wishes were answered, and the next day she went into labour. Having had three Caesarean sections previously – one of which went badly wrong – as well as one natural birth, she opted for a second natural delivery.

Labour itself was smooth and quick, and Freddie was soon born. However, to everyone's astonishment – and despite having a strong heartbeat – he didn't breathe. His blood oxygen was critically low, but there was no evidence of cord compression – the signs just didn't add up.

"Freddie was bagged and resuscitated very quickly, and made a whimpering sound, but was rushed to SCBU whilst the delivery was finished. When I next saw him, he was ventilated."

The next few hours saw Freddie's condition improve and then worsen in a cycle of agonising peaks and troughs. Within twelve hours he was breathing by himself, but then suffered fits. Nothing about him made sense: his condition, his response to drugs, his blood results, his brain wave patterns. He seemed remarkably well, just neither awake nor able to swallow easily. At times the hospital staff began to believe that he would go home as a tube fed child; but the trepidation that Merry had experienced throughout her pregnancy remained with her.

On the morning of his tenth day, Freddie developed a chest infection and his blood salts plummeted. Merry knew, in her heart of hearts, that it was over.

"Prior to a brief period where he had been awake and looking at us, we had made a 'Do Not Resuscitate' decision," she says. "Most of the health professionals felt we were being a little defeatist, but I was extremely sure I did not want to make him fight to survive for a life of disability."

Later that day, Freddie's condition deteriorated significantly; Merry and Max spent the night holding their son and hoping upon hope that the antibiotics he had been given would produce a miracle. The next morning they chose to remove his ventilation to see if he would make an effort to breathe without it, but he made no attempt to fight for life and died peacefully in the arms of his parents half an hour later.

In the weeks and months that followed Freddie's death, Merry and Max experienced a whirling concoction of emotions, but never once felt rage – something which they attribute to the outstanding care given by the hospital staff. They have since raised over £2,000 for the hospital through their toy shop, as well as sending them memorial gifts and sibling support packs.

"They were absolutely fabulous," smiles Merry, "and we couldn't have asked for more love, care and thought than they gave us. From their support through planning the delivery and labour, to the behaviour of doctors, paediatricians, nurses and midwives afterwards, we felt incredibly supported."

In fact, the SCBU nurses, midwives and doctors who cared so tenderly for Freddie during his eleven short days of life felt so close to him that they asked to attend his funeral. They were joined by one or two others. Family were not invited; Max and Merry felt that it would be too difficult for their four daughters to attend, and as such made the decision not to invite any family members for the funeral itself.

"Somehow the idea of accommodating the needs of others felt too hard," explains Merry. "A service for a baby almost nobody met felt wrong, and family without the girls felt wrong."

Merry describes the funeral as "beautiful", and gained much more peace from it than she thought she would. She and Max both wrote letters to Freddie: Max read his after carrying his son's coffin, and spoke of the wonderful life his son would have had.

"No parents could have given you more love and support than your mother and me. No brother could have been better loved and cared for than you would have been by your four sisters. You never would have been short of someone to play with, to talk with, to be cuddled by, and to be inspired by."

He focussed on the small yet wonderful moments that he had shared with his son: the comfort that Freddie took when in his parents' arms, how he seemed to relax and look as if he felt safe when he was being held. And he remembers that short time when Freddie opened his eyes and looked into his: "That moment we shared together, father and son."

In being able to remember the special moments, Merry describes her husband as her inspiration. "Since Freddie died he has kept me very grounded, reminding me at times that my viewpoint is becoming clouded and confused, and reminding me to keep enjoying what we do have."

Merry, too overcome with grief to speak, had her letter read by the chaplain. In it she yearns for the life her son should have had, and longs for the memories never to be realised.

"I want to show your beautiful, peaceful face to everyone and laugh at how, as it turns out, I rather like being a mummy to a boy after all," she writes. "I wanted to see you walk in front of me, holding your sisters' hands. I wanted to see you run and hear you shout. I never thought that motherhood could be reduced to being desperate to see you open your eyes, or being grateful forever for the times that you did. The look in your eyes when you did has been scalded into my heart.

"I wanted to tell you that you might have come last in the family, five years after the others, but that you were the most considered, the most planned, the most thought about of all our babies. I wanted a miracle for you, but I also wanted what was best for you – and from the very first moment of your life, what was best for you was not what I had planned. I want to tell you that I can remember every cuddle we had together and treasure them all."

As well as being supported and comforted by Max, Merry also drew strength from a group of close friends. It transpired that six of them had experienced a similar loss, and seeing that they had grown to cope with the pain gave Merry belief that she could do the same. A nurse told her, in the days following Freddie's death, that she and Max had handled his short life with great dignity; words which helped Merry, and gave her a desire to make her son proud of her.

Merry's advice to other parents who find themselves enduring the tragedy of losing a child is simple: "Talk, talk, talk talk. Make time to talk. We went out to lunch once a month; we'd walk first to a special place and say anything we needed to say, and then recuperate with lunch afterwards. It was hard, but essential.

"I also think it is vital not to get hung up on how the other person grieves, and compare it to your own. Max is a far more uncomplicated person than me; he doesn't belittle Freddie's loss in any way, but he is simply a person who does not mourn for what he cannot have. After the initial shell-shock wore off, he just moved on. That was hard for me, very hard, but I did understand him by then. He made a lot of time for me to grieve as I needed to."

*

Shortly after Freddie's death, Merry and Max made the difficult decision to try again for a baby: "as much for our sanity in facing babies (and future grandchildren) as anything else."

It took a "gut-wrenching" thirteen months, but Merry is now pregnant with her sixth child. When she first found out, she felt a number of emotions: relief, thrill, terror, sickness. Max was happy when he found out – Merry notices that he was perhaps the happiest he has been about any of them – but they are both very cautious, and taking each day as it comes, as Merry explains.

"It wasn't the momentous moment it might seem it should be, really. We'd tried so much that year, and then when it happened it just felt like 'Oh'."

Fortunately, the pregnancy has progressed smoothly so far, save for a slight blip during an early scan when nothing could be seen: "Typical that a reassurance scan scares the life out of you!" laughs Merry. She does not have the sense of foreboding that she had with Freddie, and in any case is resolute to stay positive for the sake of her daughters. Again, her hospital has been a pillar of support, providing counselling, sympathetic carers and regular scans.

A year after Freddie's death, Merry and Max held a memorial day for their son. "I wanted to do something," she says. "I did feel that in having such a small funeral we had missed that emotional goodbye among people to talk nonsense with us afterwards. I did want to do something, and it always felt that his birthday would be the right time for that."

Merry struggled to organise the day, and spent most of her time fretting about the weather. However, a week before the day was held, it all fell into place. She went to a party shop and bought blue balloons to which her daughters tied labels. Speculatively, Merry let her friends and family know what they were doing, and asked them to come if they wanted to and could. They came, in their droves.

"I didn't want to drag people through my process," recalls Merry, "so there were no speeches, no elaborate things, nothing to make anyone shuffle."

Instead, they counted down and let the balloons go and rise, winding their way into the grey, cloudy sky, carrying messages to her son. Afterwards, she, Max and her friends talked and laughed, and agreed that they had done the right thing. That evening they lit candles all round the garden and on the doorstep, and left them to burn until they went out. "It looked beautiful. We had sparklers too: it felt joyful, rather than sad, to do that – and is a little link between him and Josie, our Bonfire Night girl who didn't get long enough as a big sister."

And, on Merry's windowsill, sat three candles, which burned for twelve nights – one for each night their son was alive.

Early Death

Adapted to suit Freddie, and read at his funeral

He slipped away like morning dew
Before the sun was high;
So brief his time, he scarcely knew
The meaning of a sigh.

As round the rose its soft perfume,
Sweet love around him floated;
Admired he slept – while mortal doom
Crept on, unfeared, unnoted.

Love was his guardian Angel here,
Though Love to Death resigned him;
But in our thoughts and hearts he's near
And seeking there, we find him.

Matthew

It was a pub crawl which originally brought Sue and Steve together – no surprise, really, as they met at university. Being students and having little money perhaps accounts for their most memorable date being cheese and biscuits in Sue's bedroom.

In fact, they were in bed when Steve proposed, and they married in Bristol Registry Office – a day which they deliberately organised to cost less than £1,000, but was marked by "lots of friends and a Ceilidh barn dance band". Their honeymoon was spent skiing in Bulgaria: "cheap and wonderful, and as it was under Communist rule the food menu was interesting... you only got what was available, which means plenty of eggs for us as vegetarians!"

Sue and Steve had always wanted children, and four years after their wedding day Sue fell pregnant with their first child. Like many first-time mothers, she was advised not to smoke or drink alcohol, to eat well and keep fit. Also, like many mothers, she was offered an amniocentesis to check whether her baby had Down's Syndrome.

Sue enjoyed a trouble free pregnancy without even a hint of morning sickness. At thirty-eight weeks, she gave birth to a son, Chris, after an eight-hour labour. A stressful time, you might think, but Sue and Steve coped well: "playing cards and listening to Vivaldi's Four Seasons. It was very natural and relaxed."

Now a "wonderfully hairy eighteen-year-old" after being bald for the first two years of his life, Chris is anything but a grumpy teenager. "He has always had a wonderful ability to hold a conversation with anyone," says Sue, "and has a wide group of friends – most of whom party at our house!"

Almost two years after Chris was born, Sue and Steve discovered that they were to become parents for a second time. They decided on a home birth, having not enjoyed being in hospital previously and keen on establishing a relationship with the midwife who delivered their baby.

Sue's pregnancy progressed well, and she describes herself as "happy and healthy". On Saturday 30th September 1995, at thirty-eight weeks, she went into labour, and the home birth began. They rang for the midwife twice but struggled to contact her, it being the age before mobile phones; in the end, a different midwife arrived to help deliver Sue and Steve's baby whilst Steve's parents helped settle Chris into bed.

"She was lovely, but it wasn't what we'd planned," recalls Sue. "It was clear that by this time I was advanced in labour, so she asked me to get on the bed to assess me. It was at this point that she couldn't find a heartbeat."

Remaining calm and professional, the midwife blamed the monitor's batteries for the lack of heartbeat, and carried out an internal examination. Sue was ten centimetres dilated, and ready to deliver. Sue clearly remembers what happened next.

"She suggested that she break my waters, and it was at this point that Steve recalls her colour completely draining from her face. As she broke my waters there was thick, fresh meconium. She said nothing except 'Sue, we need to get this baby out, push.'"

"The pram was down from the loft," says Steve, "the nursery

was ready, we were full of anticipation, looking forward to our second child."

Twenty minutes later, Matthew arrived – but, tragically, he was stillborn. Years later, Steve would give a presentation at the British launch of *The Lancet's* international series of papers on stillbirth in April 2011, in which he spoke in vivid detail of their nightmare.

"Sue was ashen white," he said, "totally devastated, desperately rocking Matthew in her arms. I'd never seen her like that before; we'd been through a lot, but nothing like this. I was in shock, and in denial. My head buzzed, I floated around coldly telling everyone 'It's stillborn'.

"'Stillborn' is a word I'd never before even considered, let alone think about its full meaning."

Steve went on to describe what happened in the hours that followed as "an unreal series of events". Doctors visited, and an ambulance took Matthew and his stricken parents to the hospital where they filled out forms and Sue underwent checks. They returned home in the early hours of the morning, still in shock and denial.

"It wasn't until Monday, when I was putting the pram back into the loft, that my emotion and the full realisation of what had happened finally caught up with me," Steve continues. "I thought: 'Why am I putting this pram back in the loft? I should be pushing Matthew around in it, like I did with Christopher. Matthew should be here with us now."

Sue and Steve arranged to see Matthew in the hospital chapel two days later. Steve ran up to the crib and held his son in his arms for the first and last time. "I completely broke down and poured all my emotion into the child in my arms. I look back and have no idea how we got through those first few days, weeks and months. The emotional chasm between the anticipation and excitement of a new baby to the reality of a stillborn was totally overwhelming."

The grief-stricken parents requested a post-mortem, which came back inconclusive: 'an accident in the womb', with no logical explanation or reason for why Matthew died. "It made Matthew's death even more senseless and difficult to accept," says Sue.

The funeral took place at the local crematorium, organised by the hospital. The chaplain led a thoughtful service, during which she read a short poem Steve had written for his son. Only a few people attended: grandparents, as well as the midwife who delivered Matthew and their community midwife.

"It seemed right that they were there, as they had met our Matthew," explains Sue. "We made our own flower arrangements with greenery from the garden and all stood close to the coffin, not wanting to be distant in the pews. There was no music or hymns, and it only lasted about ten minutes. It was heartbreaking and yet I was numb at the same time. My mum's reaction to the tiny white coffin is one I'll never forget."

The tragedy that Sue and Steve were experiencing brought them closer, and for the first few weeks and months following Matthew's death they barely left each other's side, although they grieved differently and in different ways. Sleep provided a momentary escape, before they awoke and remembered what had happened.

Chris – who was two-and-a-half years old at the time – was not really affected by his brother's death but was deeply affected by his parents' sadness, and when he commented that "this house is too sad for me" Sue and Steve realised that they needed to grieve in a different way. Through the support of friends and family – who send flowers and parcels of food, as well as lending words of encouragement – they openly spoke about Matthew to Chris, a trait which has continued to this day.

The reaction of others was mostly generous and helpful, although Sue found that some people would pretend that it hadn't happened, or attempt to 'fix' her before she was ready. Some made misplaced and unintentionally hurtful comments: "God takes all the best children"; "I thought you were carrying high"; "You're young, you can have another." Others would cross the road to avoid speaking to her, when all she and Steve wanted to do was talk about their son.

Sue felt an overriding sense of worthlessness and failure in the dark months which followed the loss of her son. "I was always someone who felt I could achieve and cope, but this completely and absolutely floored us both."

They both needed help, and found it – along with support and empathy – in Sands, for which Sue now works as a Group Development Manager.

*

Sue and Steve desperately wanted another child, but wrestled with the decision as to whether or not to try. Matthew's inconclusive post-mortem had given them no reassurance, no reasons for his death, and so they could never be certain that the same tragedy would not happen a second time. But in the same vein, they did not want Chris to be an only child, and were aware that they were both getting older.

In the end, they decided to try again, and Sue soon fell pregnant with their third child: a discovery which brought a mixture of feelings. "I was nervous, worried, anxious... I wasn't able to focus on much else. I was constantly checking for blood in the initial months, and then checking for movement as the pregnancy progressed."

Fortunately, the hospital staff and midwives – aware of Sue's history – were very supportive, and provided many appointments with a consultant, who listened to their fears and answered their questions. He provided no guarantees, but reassured them that he would do his very best to ensure the weeks and months passed without difficulty. However, Sue and Steve still refused to believe that all would be well until their baby was alive and well in their arms.

"We suppressed all of the normal joy and expectation," remembers Sue. "We bought nothing at all – not even a nappy."

At thirty-five weeks, Sue suffered a bit of backache, and felt "odd". They rang the hospital, who suggested that she waited for a while to see if the strange feeling wore off. Steve, though, was insistent, and so they went into hospital to be checked.

They discovered that Sue was in very early labour, and she was monitored closely. All seemed to be calm, until the monitor showed that their baby's heartbeat was becoming irregular. They were rushed to a delivery suite, where – after a "very scary" delivery – Isabel was born, weighing 5lb 13oz, but alive and well. She spent a few weeks in special care, where she was cared for by "brilliant" members of staff before being able to go home.

Every year, on Matthew's birthday, Sue and Steve take the day off work and do something special. When he died some close friends bought them a candlestick, which at the time seemed a

153

bit strange, but is now lit on many occasions. They also planted a tree in his memory. Inside the house, Sue treasures the blanket onto which he was born, and the photos that they took whilst holding him in the chapel. She keeps them in a box which was made by a close family friend, in which lies a number of gifts given to them; small items which remind them of their son.

They find themselves less patient of trivial things nowadays – such as celebrities, the press or negative people – but do feel that they are better able to express and deal with their emotions, and more accepting that they cannot control what life brings. They often talk about Matthew, and wonder what he would look like now. Steve changed his middle name to Matthew, in a significant and touching gesture for the son who, in his words to *The Lancet* conference, "changed my life".

"It sounds a bit trite," says Sue, "but hopefully Matthew has made us able to search for the quality times, and celebrate them."

A Poem For Matthew

Written by Steve

Matthew.

All our hopes and dreams for your life have ended, and so we go on with our sad, heavy hearts to try to look to the future.

It's very, very hard little chap.

We have filled your soul with our love and know your soul will never die.

We will never forget you.

We will always love and cherish our beautiful little Matthew.

Scarlett

Liam and Jodie Wye are in their living room, talking about Jodie's eldest daughter, Caitlin.

"She's the grumpiest person I've ever met," laughs Liam. "Everything is down, everything is sighs. She's like Jodie, a little version of her."

A brave man, one could suggest: but, perhaps fortunately for Liam, Jodie is six months pregnant, and not really in the mood for a fight. Instead, there's just a glare, and Liam takes the hint, grinning widely.

Jodie was seven months pregnant with Caitlin when she married her first husband. She suffered with pre-eclampsia, and was going to be induced, but her waters broke at thirty-six weeks and Caitlin was born naturally. After a week in Special Care due to breathing problems, she was allowed home.

Two months later, Jodie fell pregnant again, but suffered a miscarriage – the first of six that she would have in total. "You get used to it more with each one," says Jodie. "You kind of expect it to go wrong. I'm pleasantly surprised when it doesn't, I guess."

Having read a number of books on pregnancy, Jodie was aware of the risks; but, as she says, you never think it'll happen to you. "That sort of thing always happens to someone else. Even though I had bad pregnancies, you never think anything particularly bad will happen."

After her miscarriage, Jodie fell pregnant with her son,

Morgan. In order to ease her fears, she paid for early scans during her pregnancy, and found them reassuring. Her pregnancy was not a completely smooth ride, though; she was in and out of hospital after suffering early contractions, and by the time twenty-eight weeks had passed she had been in early labour for about a week and a half. The birth itself lasted three hours, two of which were, in Jodie's words, "spent pushing."

Jodie then went on to suffer another miscarriage, at six weeks. "I guess you always think it's not fair," she says.

Not long afterwards, though, Jodie fell pregnant with Ethan whilst still with her first husband. In keeping with her previous pregnancies, this one was plagued with problems almost from the start. At twenty-two weeks her waters began to leak, which confined her to bedrest for the rest of her pregnancy, save for the weekly visit to hospital for scans, blood tests and medication. Thankfully, at thirty-four weeks the leaking stopped, and five weeks later Ethan was born.

Due to a number of reasons, Jodie and her husband separated. An avid gamer, she spent a lot of time playing *World of Warcraft* online. One day, another character asked to join her guild. His name was Liam.

"We started chatting," recalls Jodie, "and then we all met up in Leicester. That's when we fell in love."

Two years later they married, with a couple of guild members acting as witnesses. When asked about how they met each other, Liam and Jodie are noticeably embarrassed, despite it being a fascinating story. "It's even more geeky than Match.com," says Jodie. Liam squirms in his seat as Jodie recounts stories of their quests together in *World of Warcraft*: "You're not meant to say things like that out loud."

Unperturbed, Jodie gushes about Liam. "The years I've spent with Liam feel like forever, in a good way."

Jodie and Liam suffered a miscarriage in the early years of their relationship: Liam's first experience of loss. "I didn't really understand that much at first," he says. "But it wasn't a great time at all. You start thinking about baby names, and what you're going to do, and then suddenly it all stops and goes back to normal."

A year later, and after much trying, Liam and Jodie found themselves once again looking at a positive pregnancy test; Jodie was six months pregnant as she walked down the aisle towards Liam.

"It was a perfect day," she smiles. "We had our close friends and family there, and we had everything to look forward to: I remember feeling happier than ever. I thought I'd finally got through the bad times in my life and moved on. We married with music, friends and photos, and topped it off with a barbecue and drinks back at our house. It was a lovely day."

The pregnancy went smoothly, until the twenty-week abnormality scan showed that their baby had an echogenic bowel, where the intestines show up brightly on the ultrasound. "We had to have genetic tests, and they weren't sure what was causing it. We just had to wait and see."

The tests showed that Liam and Jodie were not carriers of any genetic diseases and, bizarrely, later scans did not show an echogenic bowel – which left consultants and midwives baffled.

Unfortunately, Jodie and Liam suffered from poor hospital care during their pregnancy, as Jodie explains. "They were very overworked. When we arrived for scans, they would wonder why we were there, despite us telling them on the phone minutes before. Once I went in because there was no movement, and we had to wait for two hours."

Jodie was carrying a lot of extra fluid, something which seemed to be overlooked. Her glucose level was also incredibly high, but because tests showed that she fell on the borderline for gestational diabetes, she was classed as having no problems.

To add to their concerns, their baby switched from breech to transverse regularly. One morning Jodie and Liam were on their way to hospital after having been called in due to a suspected cord prolapse, but their car – only a day old – broke down on the motorway.

Unable to continue with their journey, they waited until the following morning to receive a courtesy car and travel to the hospital. By this time, Jodie had noticed that her baby was moving much less, but was reluctant to say anything to the hospital staff.

"I'd been in so many times before I felt like I was wasting their time," she explains. Liam is quick to add his own thoughts. "Especially when the reaction they give you is rolled eyes."

Jodie was admitted to hospital and put on a trace to monitor the baby's heartbeat. However, they struggled to find one, and after a number of staff had each attempted to find a heartbeat using a handheld monitor with no success, she and Liam began to fear the worst.

"In the back of your mind, you think 'there must be something wrong'," says Jodie. "Then they called us into a room and scanned me, and told me that they couldn't find a heartbeat."

Jodie was thirty-seven weeks pregnant at the time, and the news came as a massive shock to them both. "You just feel disbelief, really. You think that it's not actually happening, and that you're going to wake up."

She and Liam were given a few minutes to absorb the terrible news, after which they were given their options. Reluctant to take any medication to induce labour, they went home and waited for it to begin naturally.

The midwife, concerned for Jodie's health, rang Liam three or four times a day asking him to persuade her to return to hospital. She was the only person that they had contact with during the few days they were at home. Jodie's parents rang friends and family to break the awful news, whilst looking after Caitlin, Morgan and Ethan. All Jodie and Liam could do was sit, wait, and try to come to terms with what had happened.

"It was winter, it was dark, and there was an overriding gloom," says Liam. Jodie explains how she felt: "I didn't want to speak to anybody. I was quite happy to sit here and pretend it wasn't happening. We just sat until we couldn't do it any more and had to go back to hospital."

Once in hospital, Jodie was induced and gave birth to Scarlett in the afternoon. The midwife took her away, cleaned and dressed her, and took some photos. Liam went into the adjoining room to the delivery suite to hold his daughter. Jodie found herself unable to face having photographs taken of her and Scarlett.

"I'd pictured beforehand that I'd hold her and do this and that, but I couldn't at the time, I just couldn't do it. I do regret it now, but I know that at that point I just couldn't deal with it."

That evening Jodie and Liam returned home after signing forms which agreed to a post-mortem. Jodie's parents organised and paid for a funeral service, right down to the flowers. Their help during Jodie and Liam's darkest hours are beyond value. "We couldn't have done it without them, not at all."

Christmas was approaching fast, and Jodie and Liam tried to get back to normal as quickly as possible for the sake of their children, all the while finding it difficult to come to terms with what had happened. One thing they noticed the most was that their lives stopped whilst others' continued.

"To you it's the most important thing that's going on," says Jodie, "but to other people it's not so much, and even if you're close to people they've got to get on with what they're doing. It's understandable in that sense, but you do notice it.

"It took a long time to sink in. You'd wake up and remember, and it'd hit you again."

Everything that they'd bought for Scarlett was put in the loft: the Moses basket, the clothes, the pram. Both Jodie and Liam dealt with their grief the same way, but at different times: Liam was the stronger at first, as Jodie "fell apart", but six months later the roles have been reversed.

Liam's overriding feeling is one of anger. Jodie has been diagnosed with gestational diabetes in her current pregnancy, and her consultant – they are now registered with another hospital – has said that it was highly likely that she also had gestational diabetes whilst pregnant with Scarlett.

The post-mortem results stated that the cause of death was hypoxia, that Scarlett was brain-damaged due to the cord being wrapped around her neck. But the results also stated that she had an immature bowel, and that her organs were enlarged, and made a point of noting that gestational diabetes could not be ruled out.

It is these facts coming to light which fuel Liam's anger, and he and Jodie plan to write a letter to the hospital stating their case. "Not a liability thing," they add, "but to help other people."

Jodie was keen to talk about Scarlett to anyone willing to lend a listening ear, and in doing so found that coming to terms with her grief came quicker than it did with Liam, who felt unable to talk about the loss of his daughter as much. They did find, however, that many people tried to avoid the subject, some to the point of ignoring that it had happened.

Fortunately, by going online and reading the stories of other parents who had suffered a similar tragedy, Jodie and Liam found a source of comfort and encouragement.

"It was helpful," explains Jodie, "because you realise that what you're feeling is normal. You feel so many different things, and it's hard to tell whether those feelings are normal, but when you realise that other people have been through the same thing, you find there's hope at the end of it.

"I always used to think 'I can't imagine ever feeling different, I'm always going to feel this way', but you do. Gradually, it gets easier to deal with."

*

Jodie and Liam were keen to have another child as soon as possible. "We weren't trying to replace Scarlett, but it was like there was something missing. You've waited all that time for a baby, and everyone was expecting it, and all of a sudden there's nothing. You come home and you've got to revert back to how you were nine months before. It's really surreal, that feeling."

Now, six months pregnant, Jodie and Liam are finding it difficult to suppress a constant feeling of anxiety. "When I found out, I was happy," says Jodie, "but also really worried. I was worried about a miscarriage, and then when you're past that stage, you worry about something else going wrong.

"I worry about everything, and I look everything up on the Internet, which often makes you more paranoid. It's helpful at some points, but it does fuel your worries."

So worried were both Liam and Jodie that they only bought the first handful of babygrows after the twenty-week scan. Now, they're feeling much more hopeful and positive.

On the first anniversary of Scarlett's birth, they bought some flowers and went to her graveside. The sombre occasion was, however, given a somewhat comical edge after a near miss with a Chinese lantern.

"We read the pack, but overlooked the bit about not lighting it in high winds," smiles Liam. "So we got it lit, but it wouldn't fly – it just rolled along the ground towards me. We had to stamp on it because it started rolling down the hill and we thought it could set fire to someone's house. We couldn't help laughing!"

Jodie and Liam have made it a tradition to buy their Christmas tree every year on Scarlett's birthday; and on their mantelpiece lays a row of candles, in memory not only of their daughter, but of the six miscarriages that Jodie has suffered. Their story is one of courage, of determination, of perseverance – but, most of all, it is one of hope.

A Poem For Scarlett

How very softly you tiptoed into our world.
Almost silently;
Only a moment you stayed.
But what an imprint your footprints have left on our hearts.

Excerpts from Letters for Scarlett

From Mummy:
"I never imagined we'd have to say goodbye to you so soon. I didn't have the strength to hold you when you were born, and I'm sorry for that, but I promise you that I will hold you in my heart and soul forever."

"I will think of and remember you always… my heart is breaking and aches with love for you, my little girl. Even though you were born sleeping you were alive and meant so much to me. You existed, you were and you still are. Nothing changes that. I love you so much more than I could ever express on this piece of paper."

From Daddy:

"I will always treasure the moments when I felt you kick and move, I will never forget how you'd make me jump and shock me with how strong you are! I will never forget your face... you are so beautiful, rightfully fitting for the little angel you have become. I love you Scarlett. I will never forget you."

"Every minute of ever hour I will think about you and pray that you're happy and safe, looking down at us. Keep your mum and brothers and sister safe, they all love and care for you more than you could imagine. I love you, my little Angel."

Chloe

Sophia Mason is no stranger to adversity. She narrowly escaped with her life after being diagnosed at the age of sixteen with Meningococcal Septicaemia, and needed to have both legs and a number of fingers amputated.

But she is a woman of action and purpose; her experiences at the hands of meningitis have prompted her to spend seventeen years campaigning for greater awareness for The Meningitis Trust, and she boasts a number of awards dedicated to her bravery and inspirational nature.

Her illness had always left a question over whether she would ever be able to have a child, but in 2009 – five months after meeting her partner on an Internet dating site – she found herself looking at a positive pregnancy test.

"Were we trying for a baby? No!" she exclaims. "When we found out we were shocked, and at the start it wasn't the happiest news."

The initial shock soon turned to joy and excitement, however, and the pregnancy itself went very well. Sophia was classed as 'low risk', and was not made aware of any warning signs to look for during the nine months of pregnancy she faced. Her pregnancy went so well, though, that it astounded the doctors who had previously told her she may never be a parent.

"They would always say I'd have swelling, and my prosthetic

legs wouldn't fit so I'd be in a wheelchair – but this never happened," she explains. "They said my organs could be put under a lot of stress again and I could get anaemia or diabetes – it never happened. I would put on lots of weight, and my back would suffer – but this also never happened.

"It was the easiest pregnancy I could have asked for: no sickness or cravings. I was fit as a fiddle and the happiest I've ever been."

At each of her checkups Sophia had perfect blood pressure, and no anomalies showed up on any scans. But she had a niggling feeling that refused to go away. Looking back, she puts this down to mother's intuition.

"I requested an elective Caesarean section," she says. "I was always worried about the birth. I wanted my baby out as quickly and as safely as possible, and to me no operation could be as bad or as painful as the amputation of my legs. I never once thought about me, I just wanted the safest delivery for my baby. That was always my priority."

One day, at twenty-seven weeks, Sophia began finding it difficult to breathe and had a terrible pain in her side. She was rushed to hospital ("we were in there for hours and hours") where it was established that 'Derek' – the name she and her partner gave her bump – had kicked her gall bladder so much it had swollen. "'Derek' moved so much – all night and all day non-stop from about fourteen weeks!"

Whilst in hospital, Sophia watched other worried parents come and go, each having been placed on a monitor for twenty minutes as they listened to the familiar muffled sound of their baby's heartbeat. By the end of the day, exhausted and frustrated, Sophia shared her annoyance with a nurse.

"I said, 'Don't you get fed up with all these women being so silly and coming up all the time?' She just laughed and said, 'Yes! It's all I do, all flippin' day!'"

Monday 30th November was ringed on Sophia and Dan's calendar: the day of her Caesarean section. Her final midwife check was on the Tuesday before, and all was fine. At the time, Sophia had noticed that her baby was moving less, and mentioned this to the midwife, who agreed with Sophia's assumption that the reduced movement was simply because of the lack of space as 'Derek' had grown.

The next day, more aware of her baby's lack of movement, Sophia became increasingly worried. 'Derek' was hardly moving at all. She spent the Thursday before her Caesarean section arranging her will, ensuring that Dan and her baby would be looked after if something happened to her on the operating table. "I was still adamant that something was going to go wrong."

For the rest of the day Sophia kept mentioning to Dan that she didn't feel right, that the baby felt heavy and hadn't moved.

"That evening I sat and had a small glass of red wine, and I purposely put the glass on my tummy," she says. "I thought if the baby moved just slightly then I'd really see it. I don't know if it was a kick or not, but the glass flew off my tummy and splattered all over our cream sofa and cream carpet – I can see the stains even now!"

Sophia's relief at the spilt wine was short-lived, and she lay awake all night poking and rubbing her baby, who previously had always moved when she did so. That night, there was nothing at all.

"At 4.30am I knew," remembers Sophia. "I felt the elbow and moved it around – there was no opposition to me doing this. Baby was not asleep; I knew it had gone."

Dan provided words of reassurance as they prepared to go into hospital, reminding her that the midwife said all was fine on Tuesday. He rang the ward to tell the nurse that the baby hadn't moved in twenty-four hours, and was shouted at for leaving it so long.

"We didn't know any different," explains Sophia, who will never forget that night. "Every story you read is the same – the drive to the hospital that seemed to take forever, the haze of nurses testing and feeling your tummy, the Doppler, the monitors, the scans and the 'Sorry'."

Sophia puts her subsequent calmness down to her mother's intuition; the fact that she had known in her heart of hearts all day that something was terribly wrong. As Dan struggled to come to terms with the news, Sophia called her parents.

"My mum was so excited; this was going to be her first grandchild. But as soon as she heard my voice and not Dan's she knew there was a problem. She said 'What's happened, Soph?' and I replied: 'My baby has died Mum, I'm so sorry.'"

Sophia then rang the hospital porter – a friend named Chris, who had seen them go into hospital – and told him what had happened. She asked him to look out for her parents, who were on their way, and to look after them for her. She then called her cousin and best friend.

"I made sure the family were looked after and all were there for my partner; I even went out to meet his family when they arrived. I was so worried about him. He'd done everything he was meant to do throughout my pregnancy: he'd reassured me and supported me. What else could he do? It was me who had to look after our baby, and I felt I had failed, I'd let him down, our family and my baby."

At 9.30am Sophia underwent a Caesarean section, and Chloe Joan was born. She was given straight to Dan and her cousin; Sophia first saw her daughter at 10.20am, when she awoke from her general anaesthetic.

"My little angel who danced too much and just got herself in a knot," she remembers fondly. "A little clumsy, just like her mummy; but the absolute image of her daddy."

The umbilical cord was wrapped around Chloe's neck twice, and the nurses said that they were 99.9% sure that this was the reason for her death. Formally, though, Chloe's death is classed as 'unexplained'.

For the weeks and months which followed the tragic death of their daughter, Sophia blamed herself.

"All I kept asking myself is 'Why didn't I listen to my instinct? Why didn't I realise she was trying to tell me she was struggling? Why didn't I realise her not kicking my gall bladder any more wasn't a good thing?'"

But the more she looked into the circumstances surrounding Chloe's death, the more Sophia found that a lack of communication had led to a lack of knowledge – and, in some cases, she was believing a complete myth.

"Why do people say 'babies don't move much towards the due date because there's no room' when this is totally untrue?" she asks. "Why were there no posters on the hospital walls or stories in the many pregnancy magazines and websites I'd spent the last nine months reading? Why didn't the midwives tell me that observing a change in movement could save her? Why do I feel such a failure?"

Since Chloe's death, Sophia has slowly but surely taken away the myth and uncovered fact. Her consultant informed her that a baby's movements do not reduce before labour – in fact, they should become more noticeable because there is less room. He also said that an increase in movement should also be treated with concern, as this could show that the baby is struggling.

Although some of Sophia's questions have been answered, her daughter is still absent. All she has to remind her of the baby she lost is a few precious items and the red wine stains on her carpet. And on the night she lost Chloe, she was not alone.

"I was shocked to find out that in the three days I was in hospital when I lost Chloe there were four families in the ward going through the same agony, feeling the same loss. Four of us lost our babies!"

Sophia felt a number of emotions during these dark days: anger, frustration, guilt, jealousy, emptiness, confusion… but also a sense of sheer determination to make a change and prevent other parents from suffering the same tragedy.

In late 2009 Sophia established COUNT THE KICKS™, an organisation which encourages expectant mothers to take responsibility for their own health and the health of their baby. It has gone from strength to strength, and has featured in a number of national newspapers and magazines.

"We want mums to be confident enough to ask questions of their healthcare providers. We want them to be armed with knowledge to prepare and empower them."

Chloe's funeral took place in early December: "a beautiful sunny day; perfect, just like her". Over 200 people attended, some of whom Sophia had never met but whose lives had been touched by the excitement of her pregnancy and the tragedy of her loss.

Dan was Sophia's rock in the weeks which followed. "He helped me stay sane," she smiles. "He kept me going, but also stopped me doing too much. He kept me occupied but also held me back.

"Losing Chloe was the making of us. She was and always will be the link between us; she pulled us together and she made sure we will stay together."

Chloe has given Sophia more in her short life than anybody else ever could. She has shown her mum that she can have a baby even though she lost her legs; that she should trust her own instincts, ask questions if she's worried, and never give up. Sophia wrote about her at the time with fondness in an article for CountTheKicks.org.uk: "She has proven to me that I will be an amazing mummy one day. She is my little Guardian, our little Angel."

*

It was ten months after Chloe's death that Sophia fell pregnant, after trying to conceive for a while. Knowing that they were pregnant made Chloe's first birthday a lot easier, and they took the opportunity to tell friends and family.

But the arrival of her second child – a son, named George – was not without drama. He was due on 15th June, and the excited parents made an appointment for a Caesarean section on the 25th May. A few days before the operation was due to take place Sophia received her first injection of steroids, to mature George's lungs. She was due to return to hospital the next day for the second injection, but that morning became worried that once more she was feeling reduced movement.

"I went through the process of trying to trigger a movement: cold drink, hot drink, chocolate, laying down, rubbing my tummy... but there was nothing. I started to worry, so called my midwife who told me to go straight to the ward. I was petrified – I thought it had happened again."

Dan – a fire-fighter – was on duty at the time, so Sophia called her best friend who drove her to the hospital immediately. Inconsolable, Sophia was placed into a wheelchair and taken through the same corridors and the same wards as she was with Chloe.

"They whisked me in and straight away got a Doppler to look for the baby's pulse," she recalls. "While they did this they were reassuring me that it can sometimes take a minute or two to find the heartbeat – it didn't help that because I was sobbing my tummy was moving."

Thankfully, and to Sophia's overwhelming relief, a heartbeat was found straight away and a monitor was strapped around Sophia's belly. But something wasn't right. Whenever Sophia experienced what the hospital staff thought was a Braxton-Hicks contraction, George's pulse rate would dip considerably.

Dan arrived at the hospital; he and Sophia decided that they would ask to stay the night. The consultant came round to check on mum and baby, at which point Sophia told him about the dipping pulse rate. He and the Senior Midwife – who had delivered Chloe and since become a close friend to Sophia and Dan – watched as another contraction came and the rate dropped.

"We all watched, unable to breathe," remembers Sophia. "The consultant stood up and walked out. Claire, the Senior Midwife, asked me 'What do you want, Sophia? Tell me what you want.'

"I just said 'I want to take my baby home in my arms alive, Claire.' She just turned away and walked out of the ward."

Within a few minutes Claire and the consultant had returned, dressed in scrubs and ready to wheel Sophia into theatre. Sophia remembers it vividly.

"Mr Koomson, the consultant, said: 'Right Sophia, we all want to meet your baby – do you?' Dan and I just stared at each other!"

There was little time to get scared, or ask questions. Sophia was changed into a gown and taken into theatre; Dan appeared a few moments later in blue scrubs, which made Sophia laugh. The theatre staff all chatted to her as an epidural was administered and the operation began. Sophia's community midwife burst into the theatre, having rushed back from a day out in London to be with them.

"At eleven minutes past eleven in the evening the consultant said 'Look who I have, Dan!'" says Sophia. "Dan looked up and then looked at me, and said 'It's a boy, Soph, we've had a boy!'"

George didn't cry, and his lips were quite dark – like Chloe's – but he opened his eyes and looked at Sophia; something, she says, that Chloe never got to do. He then frowned, yawned, and fell asleep.

The next morning Claire came to see Sophia and explained that when they delivered George they could see that her placenta was failing, which is why George's pulse was dipping. If Sophia had gone home, or lain in the ward too afraid to pester the midwives or ask questions, then she could have lost George as well.

"She also said that this was likely to have been the reason for Chloe's death, and if we choose to have another baby it will probably happen again," says Sophia. "I asked my consultant what the signs of a failing placenta are, and he said 'a reduction in movement, Sophia – you saved his life.'"

174

This dramatic experience – given a happy ending through Sophia's observation and ability to ask for help – gave her even more impetus to make a success of COUNT THE KICKS™, shifting the focus from stillbirth and loss to positivity; being aware and being confident. Today, her organisation helps to inform and empower mothers around the world.

The loss of Sophia and Dan's daughter has changed them. "I never take anything for granted," says Sophia, "and cherish every moment." It has given her the drive to spread knowledge of foetal movement far and wide, and help to dispel the myths surrounding pregnancy. There is no way of knowing how many lives have been saved through her campaign; but just one would count as a huge success.

And Chloe's loss has proven one thing: Sophia has indeed become an amazing mummy.

Stevie Wonder: 'Isn't She Lovely'

Played at Chloe's funeral

Isn't she lovely
Isn't she wonderful
Isn't she precious
Less than one minute old
I never thought through love we'd be
Making one as lovely as she
But isn't she lovely, made from love?

Isn't she pretty
Truly the angel's best
Boy, I'm so happy
We have been heaven blessed
I can't believe what God has done
Through us He's given life to one
But isn't she lovely, made from love?

Isn't she lovely
Life and love are the same
Life is Aisha
The meaning of her name
Londie, it could not have been done
Without you who conceived the one
That's so very lovely, made from love.

About Sands

Sands, the stillbirth and neonatal death charity, was founded in 1978 by a small group of bereaved parents devastated by the death of their babies, and by the total lack of acknowledgement and understanding of the significance and impact of their loss. Since that time we have supported many thousands of families whose babies have died, offering emotional support, comfort and practical help.

Sands today operates throughout the UK and focuses on three main areas of work:

We support anyone affected by the death of a baby

Bereavement support is at the core of everything we do. Some of the services that we offer include:
• Helpline for parents, families, carers and health professionals
• UK-wide network of support Groups with trained befrienders
• Online forum and message boards enabling bereaved families to connect with others
• Website and a wide range of leaflets, books and other resources.

We work in partnership with health professionals to try to ensure that bereaved parents and families receive the best possible care

We undertake a comprehensive programme of training, workshops and talks for health professionals based on the

Sands Guidelines which give practical guidance on how to meet parents' needs and provide good bereavement care.

We promote and fund research that could help to reduce the loss of babies' lives

In spite of medical advances, the shocking reality is that each day in the UK there are eleven babies who are stillborn and six who die within the first twenty-eight days of life. Through our Why17? campaign, we are raising vital funds for research, while challenging government to address these individual tragedies as a matter of urgency and priority.

We depend on the extraordinary energies of our supporters to raise the vital funds that we need to deliver the wide range of services that we offer.

How Sands can help you

Sands is a national charity that can offer you emotional support and practical help if your baby has died during pregnancy, at birth or shortly afterwards.

Seventeen babies are stillborn or die shortly after birth every day in the UK and each year we support thousands of families whose babies have died.

At Sands you will find people who understand what it's like, because many of us have been through this devastating experience ourselves.

You many not want anything from us right away. We are here to help whenever you feel you need it, that may be now or in a few weeks, months or even years.

As well as supporting, mothers, fathers and same sex partners, we are also here to help other members of the family, especially grandparents and other children. Many other people may be touched by your baby's death, including friends, colleagues and health care staff.

All are welcome to contact us for support and information.

Do you want to speak to someone on our helpline?
020 7436 5881

Do you want to email us for support?
helpline@uk-sands.org

Do you want to connect with others whose baby has died?
www.sandsforum.org

Do you want to find out about a Sands group local to you?
helpline@uk-sands.org

Do you want information and books to read?
www.uk-sands.org

Do you want to email us for general information?
info@uk-sands.org

Do you want to make a donation or fundraise?
fundraising@uk-sands.org

Do you want to talk to someone in Sands head office?
020 7436 7940

Do you want to write to us?
Sands, 3rd Floor
28 Portland Place,
London, W1B 1LY

Sands support resources

If you would like more information, or would like to order Sands support booklets, our *Always Loved Never Forgotten* memory boxes, our books for children and other resources, you can order these from our website or by phone. To order online please go to www.uk-sands.org/Shop.